Jug Dogs (Jugs)

Owners Guide from Puppy to Old Age

Choosing, Caring for, Grooming,
Health, Training and Understanding
Your Jug Dog

By Alan Kenworthy

Copyright and Trademarks

Disclaimer and Legal Notice

Foreword

If you have never seen a Jug dog for yourself, you are missing out on one of the most adorable and friendly new designer dog breeds out there.

A hybrid of the Pug and Jack Russell Terrier, the Jug has all of the best features of both breeds.

These little dogs are energetic and people-loving like a Jack Russell with the unique quirkiness of a Pug.

As an owner, expert trainer and professional dog whisperer, I would like to teach you the human side of the equation, so you can learn how to think more like your dog and eliminate behavioral problems with your pet.

If you are thinking about buying one of these dogs, this book is the perfect place to start.

Within the pages of this book you will find answers to all of your questions about Jugs, including those you never thought to ask!

Here you will learn the basics about the breed, its history, temperament, appearance and more, including tips for housing, training, feeding and breeding.

This book is the ultimate guide for anyone who wants to own a Jug.

Alan Kenworthy

Acknowledgments

I would like to extend my sincerest thanks to my family, who have always been supportive of me and my writing endeavors.

Special thanks to my own Jugs, Lacey and Potts, who were the inspiration for this book.

In writing this book, I also sought tips, advice, photos and opinions from many experts of the Jug breed.

In particular I wish to thank the following people for going out of their way to help and contribute:

Little Rascals Breeders

http://www.littlerascalsuk.com

Mercedes Clark-Smith

Emma Fisher & James Lawrence

John McQuillan

Tim Webb

Jimtography

Christy Gallois

Barbra Baker

Table of Contents

Table of Contents

Table of Contents

Table of Contents

Table of Contents

Chapter 1 - History and Origins of the Breed

Photo Credit: Sergei by Mercedes Clark-Smith

Introduction

What happens when you cross a Pug with a Jack Russell Terrier? The answer is not the punchline to a joke, but the name of a new designer dog breed – the Jug.

Jug dogs are a hybrid of the Pug and Jack Russell breeds, blessed with the best traits of both parent breeds and a giant heart to boot. These little dogs are full of love and energy, which makes them a great breed for both singles and families.

Within the pages of this book, you will find valuable information about this wonderful breed, covering topics including buying a Jug, caring for your Jug and preparing for potential health problems.

You will receive detailed information about the history of the breed, as well as its appearance and temperament – you will also receive in-depth tips and instructions for training your Jug.

A true Jug consists of 50% of each – meaning that one parent must be a purebred Jack Russell Terrier and the other a purebred Pug.

It is also possible, however, to breed an existing Jug dog back to one of the parent breeds. This will result in a Jug having more Pug or Jack Russell Terrier blood, but it will still be a Jug dog.

Given the fact that Jugs are a hybrid of two different breeds, the key to understanding what a Jug is like is to understand a little more about Pugs and Jack Russell Terriers.

How Is a Jug Different From Other Dogs?

The truth of the matter is that all dog breeds are different – that is why they are given different names and used for different purposes.

Though the many dog breeds we know today were likely developed from a smaller pool of breeds through years of crossbreeding and hybridization, every dog breed is unique.

What makes the Jug breed different from many existing breeds, however, is the fact that it can only be achieved by breeding together purebreds of two different breeds – the Pug and Jack Russell Terrier.

In addition to giving it a unique appearance, this hybridization creates a dog with a mash-up of the personality traits of both breeds.

The Jack Russell Terrier

The Jack Russell Terrier is a small and compact dog with a great deal of energy and a fun-loving personality. These little dogs are very intelligent and fearless – they can be trained for tasks that they will perform with the utmost dedication.

As suggested by the name, Jack Russell Terriers belong to the Terrier group and, like many dogs their size, they have an average lifespan between 10 and 15 years.

These little dogs are charming and fun to own, but they can be a little challenging at times. In this section, you will learn the basics about the Jack Russell Terrier breed, including its history and characteristics.

Physical Characteristics

As a terrier, the Jack Russell Terrier is a fairly small dog. This breed tends to reach an average height around 10 to 15 inches (25 to 38 cm) and a weight between 14 and 18 lbs. (6 to 8 kg).

Depending on breeding, some Jack Russells stand only 10 to 12 inches (25 to 30 cm), which makes the length of their bodies greater than their height – these dogs are referred to as Shorty Jacks.

In some ways, these dogs more closely resemble Dachshunds than Jack Russell Terriers due to their elongated body shape. In terms of appearance, the Jack Russell Terrier has a compact body with short, muscular legs.

The eyes are dark and almond-shaped, while the ears are V-shaped and small. These dogs have drop ears that are carried forward and close to the head.

The tail is carried high and typically measures about 4 inches (10 cm) long, though it is sometimes docked.

The coat of this breed is smooth and predominantly white in color with tan, brown or black markings.

There are three different coat types – smooth, rough or broken (a combination of smooth and rough). Rough-coated Jack Russell Terriers have long hair, while smooth-coated varieties have a short, smooth coat.

Personality and Temperament

The Jack Russell Terrier breed is widely known for being energetic and playful. Because they are so energetic, this breed requires plenty of daily exercise and does best when given a yard to run and play in.

Socialization is also incredibly important for this breed because these dogs tend to develop "small dog syndrome" – the tendency to become dominant and strong-willed.

Dogs that are not properly socialized at a young age may develop problems with aggression around other dogs and may not be adaptable to new situations later in life.

As family pets, Jack Russell Terriers tend to get along well with people. These dogs do best in an environment where there is a set routine, especially when it comes to training.

Though they thrive on structure, Jack Russell Terriers can become bored with repetition, so it is best to keep training sessions short.

This breed tends to do well with various dog sports such as flyball and agility – these sports will also give the dog a means of working off its excess energy, which will help prevent the development of problem behaviors.

In the home, Jack Russell Terriers are generally friendly toward children. It is important to teach children how to properly handle the dog, however, because this breed is not tolerant of rough handling.

Jack Russells should not be trusted with small animals because they have a strong prey drive and are likely to chase cats and other household pets.

This breed is not recommended for apartments or small dwellings unless care is taken to provide the dog with adequate daily exercise outside the home.

Breed History

The development of the Jack Russell Terrier breed is credited to Reverend John Russell, a parson and hunter born in the late 1700s.

The origins of the breed can be traced back to the English White Terrier, a breed that is now extinct, but was used to provide the

Jack Russell Terrier with its characteristic white coat and diminutive size.

In 1819, Reverend John Russell came across a white-and-tan female terrier named Trump that he used to start his breeding program. Russell's goal was to create a small terrier that had high stamina and the courage needed to bolt foxes that had gone to ground.

By the 1850s, the breed Reverend John Russell had begun to develop was recognized as a separate breed.

Following the Reverend's death, two men by the names of East and Archer continued to develop the breed. East used dogs that were directly descended from Russell's dogs and, through selective breeding, he aimed for a type that was smaller than the typical show Fox Terrier, which weighed in around 15 lbs. (6.8kg).

In 1894, the first standard for the breed was written by Arthur Blake Heinemann, the founder of the Devon and Somerset Badger Club. The aim of this club was to promote badger digging instead of fox hunting, and Heinemann used dogs that were likely descended from Russell's own line in his breeding program.

During the 20th century, the club was renamed the Parson Jack Russell Terrier Club. Around this time, bull terrier blood was introduced into the breeding stock to strengthen the breed – this is thought to have led to the shorter-legged variety of Jack Russell Terrier that appeared during the early 20th century.

There was also around this time a great deal of variety in terriers carrying the Jack Russell name. Some dogs were bred larger for show, while others were bred small and strong for hunting.

After World War II, the need for hunting terriers declined and so too did the popularity of the Jack Russell Terrier breed.

During this time, the breed was crossed with Chihuahuas, Welsh Corgis and other small terriers to create a smaller companion dog – these dogs became known as Russell Terriers or Shorty Jacks (some even acquired the nickname Puddin' Dogs).

In 1976, the Jack Russell Terrier Club of America was formed by Ailsa Crawford.

In the years that followed, standards for the breed were firmly established, and a number of other breed clubs sprang up throughout the UK.

Clubs that sought to develop the breed's working abilities continued to identify the breed as the Jack Russell Terrier, while

American show types came to carry the name Parson Russell Terrier.

Pugs

The Pug is another small breed dog known for its wrinkled skin and curled tail.

These little dogs are typically fawn or black in color, though even the fawn-colored Pugs have black markings on the ears and face.

The body of this breed is compact and sturdy with strong legs and a short, blunt muzzle.

Pugs have large, dark eyes and small ears that are rose or button-shaped.

Physical Characteristics

Pugs are a small breed of dog classified as a companion dog. The Pug grows to a height between 10 and 14 inches (25 to 36 cm) and typically weighs between 13 and 20 lbs. (6 to 9 kg). These dogs have an average lifespan between 12 and 15 years, though they are prone to certain health problems that may reduce their lifespan. Some common health problems affecting the breed include epilepsy, hip dysplasia and obesity.

Pugs have short, smooth coats that are typically fawn-colored or black. Though the coat of this breed may be short, it is double-coated, which means that it may shed significantly, particularly during the summer. Regular brushing and monthly bathing is recommended to help control shedding for this breed.

Nail trimming is also essential because these dogs are not highly active, so their nails may not be worn down naturally by outdoor activity.

The physical characteristics for which Pugs are most well-known include the breed's bulging eyes, wrinkled face and curled tail.

Pugs have large, dark eyes and a flattened face with deep-set wrinkles.

The skin on the Pug's body is fairly loose and the body has a thickset, robust frame.

The ears of this breed are typically folded and triangular in shape – because they are folded, this breed is prone to ear infections if the ears are not kept clean and dry.

Personality and Temperament

Pugs are known for their animated spirit and their happy-go-lucky attitude. These dogs are loyal and affectionate with family, and they are eager to please.

Though the Pug is highly intelligent, they become bored easily – if your Pug is not properly trained, he may develop problem behaviors like chewing or digging.

Pugs can also be fairly strong-willed, so firm and consistent training is needed to keep these dogs under control.

Training will also help to prevent the Pug's tendency to become jealous of other dogs and children – this jealousy can cause the dog to develop guarding behaviors for food, toys and certain locations in the house.

This breed is fairly inactive indoors, so they are well adapted to apartment life and do not necessarily need a yard.

Housetraining for this breed can be difficult because Pugs have a tendency to be a little stubborn – for this reason, crate training is recommended.

In regard to their noise level, Pugs do not tend to be yappy, though they will raise the alarm if someone approaches the house, which makes them good watchdogs.

Breed History

The Pug breed is widely recognized as one of the oldest breeds of dog, though its origins are up for debate. The breed is thought to have originated prior to 400 BC, likely in Asia, where it may have descended from a type of short-haired Pekingese.

Other theories suggest that the Pug descended from a small Bulldog or that it may be a miniature form of the Dogue de Bordeaux.

Though the exact origins of the breed are unknown, it is known that the breed came into popularity during the Song Dynasty in China, during which time they were also imported into Europe.

During the 16th and 17th centuries, the Pug breed became a fixture in European courts. It is said to have been the official dog of the House of Orange during the 1570s, when a Pug named Pompey reportedly saved the Prince's life by alerting him to the approach of assassins.

It is also thought that, during the late 1600s, the Pug breed was crossed with the King Charles Spaniel, which may be why modern specimens of the breed display some Pug-like characteristics.

During the 18th century, the popularity of the Pug breed increased greatly when Queen Victoria became a fan. The Queen bred Pugs herself and helped to establish the Kennel Club in 1873.

Portraits of European royalty during the 1800s can be seen to feature many Pugs, including those owned by King George V and King Edward VIII. In 1886, Lady Brassey, a British aristocrat, brought several black Pugs back from China, which sparked the popularity of this breed variation.

Around the same time, the Pug breed was introduced in the United States and was recognized by the American Kennel Club in 1885. The Pug Dog Club of America was formed in 1931, and fifty years later, the first Pug won the Westminster Kennel Club Dog Show.

Facts About Jug Dogs

Now that you know a little more about the parent breeds of the Jug dog, you have a foundation on which to build your understanding of the Jug breed.

The first thing you will notice about the Jug dog is its unique appearance. Because the Pug and Jack Russell Terrier breeds are so different from each other in appearance, it stands to reason that a hybrid of the two will look very unique.

Jug dogs actually exhibit a fairly even blend of the two breeds – they have a small body frame with a lighter build than a Pug but a hefty conformation like that of a Jack Russell Terrier.

The most obvious evidence of its Pug parentage, however, is the squashed face and the curled tail, though not all Jugs possess these traits – it largely depends on breeding. Some Jugs exhibit a more elongated facial structure like that of the Jack Russell Terrier.

In terms of coat and color, Jugs exhibit a great deal of variation depending on breeding. Jack Russell Terriers alone can produce three different coat types (smooth, rough or broken), which, when combined with the short smooth coat of the Pug, yields a variety of results.

Jugs that are bred from rough-coated Jack Russell Terriers typically have longer hair, particularly on the face.

If both parent dogs have smooth coats, the resulting litter of Jugs will likely have the short, smooth coat of a Pug, possibly with the slightly longer fur of the Jack Russell Terrier.

Regarding temperament, the Jug maintains the intelligence of both parent breeds, as well as their lively and outgoing natures. These little dogs are fairly energetic, requiring plenty of daily exercise and playtime to keep their minds and bodies actively engaged.

Jug dogs are generally affectionate with people, but they can be a little stubborn – this breed is particularly prone to developing "small dog syndrome," so a firm and consistent hand in training is required, as well as proper socialization from a young age.

Because this breed is very intelligent, however, training is generally not a problem.

Why Breed Jug Dogs?

If you have never encountered the Jug breed before, you may be wondering why anyone would want to cross the Jack Russell Terrier and Pug breeds. The reason for crossing any two breeds of dog is simple – to create the ideal combination of physical and temperamental characteristics.

In crossing the Jack Russell Terrier and Pug breeds, you are left with a small-breed dog that is ideal for apartment life as a companion pet.

Photo Credit: Jimtography

Jugs typically exhibit a combination of the best characteristics of both breeds, including the following:

- Small size from both Jack Russell and Pug breeds

- Smooth, short coat of the Pug (may be a little longer depending on Jack Russell parentage)

- Affectionate and friendly with family (combination of both breeds)

- Very intelligent and trainable -- from the Jack Russell breed

- Loving disposition, craves time with family from the Pug breed

- Some level of hunting instinct from the Jack Russell breed

- Attractive combination of colors from both breeds

As is true with any dog, regardless of whether it is a purebred or a hybrid breed, the individual characteristics and temperament may vary depending on parentage and breeding.

With Jugs, the physical characteristics in regard to the facial and body structure, as well as coat length and color, can vary greatly from one litter to another.

In terms of personality and temperament, however, the Jack Russell and Pug breeds are fairly compatible, so a Jug will exhibit the best qualities of both breeds.

Breeding: hybrid of Pug and Jack Russell Terrier

Weight: 12 to 16 lbs. (5 to 7 kg)

Height: 10 to 14 inches (25 to 36 cm)

Lifespan: 12 to 15 years

Coat: short and smooth or broken (depends on type of coat Jack Russell Terrier parent has)

Colors: varied; generally fawn, caramel, tan or black

Eyes: large and brown

Ears: thin and dropped

Face: typically short muzzle and wrinkled face, may have a slightly elongated snout depending on Jack Russell lineage

Tail: typically curled and carried over the back

Temperament: lively, outgoing, friendly, affectionate with family

Strangers: can be protective if not properly socialized

Other Dogs: can be aggressive if not properly socialized

Training: very intelligent, responds well to firm and consistent training (best if started early)

Energy: fairly high energy, requires regular daily exercise

History of Jugs as Pets

The exact origins of the Jug dog breed are not very well documented, but it is generally accepted that the breed was developed in the United States, possibly as far back as the 1960s.

It is unknown whether the first breeding was planned or accidental but, since the 1960s, the Jug breed has risen in popularity throughout the U.S. and in the U.K.

Today there are several enthusiast clubs in both the U.S. and the U.K. devoted to this wonderful breed and its dedicated owners.

American Canine Hybrid Club
http://www.achclub.com/modules.php?name=Breeders

International Designer Canine Registry
http://designercanineregistry.com/

Designer Breed Registry
http://www.designerbreedregistry.com/

Mixed Breed Dog Clubs of America
http://mbdca.tripod.com/

The International Designer Canine Registry

Though the Jug breed is not eligible for registration or show with the AKC (American Kennel Club), you can register your Jug with the International Designer Canine Registry (IDCR).

This organization is the world's premier designer dog registry, which was started to provide registration and pedigree services exclusively to designer dog breeds.

The mission statement of the IDCR includes three points:

•   "To be consistently recognized in the canine community as a professional organization that manages a vibrant, progressive, dependable and responsible designer breed specific registry"

•   "To maintain a registry exclusively for designer/hybrid dogs and preserve the integrity of the IDCR's genetic database"

•   "To be clearly recognized and respected by the canine community as an organization that truly cares about the advancement and betterment of all canines"

Registering your Jug with the IDCR provides a number of benefits. In addition to becoming part of a community that appreciates and respects hybrid breeds, registering with the IDCR provides a means for recording your dog's ancestry.

This is particularly important if you plan to breed your Jugs. Even those who do not breed their dogs, however, enjoy having a record of their pet's lineage.

Chapter 2 - What to Know Before You Buy

Without question, Jugs are adorable. For many people, it's an instant attraction, but I'm actually not a big fan of adopting a dog on the basis of "window shopping."

You need to learn everything you can about the breed — which you are clearly doing by reading this book — and preferably spend some time with Jugs before you make your decision.

Never adopt any breed until you know, as much as it is possible to do so, what living with the dog will be like. That includes exploring all of the possible parameters of an adoption to make the right choice.

Photo: Rocky the Jug

Do You Need a License?

Before you bring your Jug home, you need to think about whether there are any licensing restrictions in your area.

Some countries have strict licensing requirements for the keeping of particular animals, so you need to check to be sure whether you need one for your Jug.

Even if you are not legally required to have a license for your Jug, you might still want to consider getting one. Having a license for your dog means that there is an official record of your ownership so, should someone find your dog if he gets lost, they will be able to find your contact information and reconnect you with him.

There are no federal regulations in the United States regarding the licensing of dogs, but most states do require that dogs be licensed by their owners, otherwise you may be subject to a fine.

Fortunately, dog licenses are inexpensive and fairly easy to obtain – you simply file an application with the state and then renew the license each year. In most cases, licensing a dog costs no more than $25.

How Many Should You Buy?

The answer to this question varies depending on a number of factors. First, you have to consider whether you have the time and financial resources to care for more than one Jug dog.

Do not purchase a second dog just because you think the first one might be lonely – you should only purchase two dogs if you can give both of them the highest level of care possible.

Another factor to consider is whether Jugs can get along peacefully with other dogs. For the most part, Pugs do well with other dogs if they are properly socialized while still young. If they aren't trained well, however, Pugs can become jealous around other dogs and may start to develop aggressive or guarding behavior.

Jack Russell Terriers also have a tendency to be dominant around other dogs, especially if they are not trained or socialized early enough.

If you do choose to buy more than one Jug dog, it is best to buy both of them at the same time while they are still young. Puppies are very impressionable, and the first few months of their lives are the ideal time to introduce changes and new situations because that is when the puppy is most adaptable.

If you buy both of your Jugs at the same time and raise them together, you are unlikely to have trouble with them getting along in the future. Keep in mind, however, that proper training and socialization is necessary to ensure that your Jugs get along with other dogs.

Male or Female?

The question of male versus female is raised with every breed, and even with every species. You can easily find adherents for either gender. I personally believe that the real shaping factors in any dog's personality are its early socialization and existing environment.

Puppy or Adult?

Adult dogs are typically adopted through a rescue group. I am a strong advocate for the work these people do, and I believe in rescue adoptions. With some breeds, however, that may only be the best choice for an experienced dog owner, not someone "meeting" the breed for the first time.

Adult dogs typically come with their own "baggage," which won't be a deal breaker for someone who knows and understands dogs. If a Jug has, for instance, not proven to be good with other pets, and you have no other animals, that anti-social streak can be managed.

There are, of course, advantages that go along with adopting an adult dog. You will know the animal's exact size and how well it will fit into your home, and you'll have a good idea of its exercise needs almost immediately. Older dogs also tend to be calmer, and they will already be housebroken.

You do have to be careful with rescue adoptions, however. Try to determine how many homes the Jug has had. If the dog has just been with one other owner, you shouldn't have a problem bonding, but dogs that have been with one family after another will have difficult issues.

It's also possible to get a dog that has been extremely dependent on its former owner and is suffering from severe separation anxiety or, in the case of owner death, genuine grief. Often crate training can alleviate this type of issue by giving the dog a safe "den" when you are away.

Younger dogs (less than two years of age) adopted from shelters can have any of these problems, although they do tend to adapt fairly quickly. Always find out if a younger dog has been given up due to a housebreaking issue.

Cases of severe separation anxiety that have led to various "bad" behaviors also cause many dogs to be given up. These may include barking, digging, chewing, or soiling the house. Crate training is also useful in these instances, but the help of a professional dog trainer may be necessary.

For first-time Jug owners, the best option is, in my opinion, to adopt a puppy from a reputable breeder. You will not only be assured of getting a healthy pet, but you will have an expert to turn to in your first days of "parenthood," when you may well need some advice.

You and your dog will grow up together, in essence, and from an early age the Jug will learn your habits and routines. You will be faced with the challenges of housebreaking and other necessities of ushering a puppy into adulthood, but the reward will be a dog that knows you and your household intimately.

Can Your Jug Be Kept With Other Pets?

Whether or not your Jug dog can be kept with other pets largely depends on individual personality. Some dogs can be completely calm and trustworthy around cats and small pets, while others simply cannot.

Photo Credit: Frank by Tim Webb

The problem with Jugs is that they are part terrier, and terriers are known for having a high prey drive. This being the case, Jugs may not get along with cats and other smaller household pets. Again, however, it depends on the individual dog's temperament.

If you do plan to keep your Jug dog with other pets, it would be wise to introduce them while they are still young.

When your dog is still a puppy is the easiest time to get him used to new things like cats or other household pets – if he grows up learning that the cat is not something he is allowed to chase, you are less likely to have problems with it later down the road.

It would also be wise for you to train your Jug dog to respond to an "Off" or "Leave it" command – the type of command you would use to get him to drop a toy or another object.

Purchase Price

Before you bring your Jug dog home, it is essential that you determine whether you can handle the financial responsibility of keeping a dog. Owning a dog can be expensive.

The initial costs for a Jug dog include the cost to purchase the dog as well as initial vaccinations, spay/neuter surgery, microchipping, and various accessories.

The most important initial cost you must consider when buying a Jug is, of course, the cost of the dog itself. Costs for Jugs may vary depending on where you look – you may be able to find one at your local pet store, though you should not expect that to be the case, since Jugs are still fairly rare.

Your best bet is to buy from a local or regional breeder who specializes in the Jug breed – just be careful not to fall victim to the misconception that hybrid breeds like Jugs should be more expensive than purebred dogs.

You should expect to pay between $200 and $800 (£130 - £500) for a Jug puppy from a reputable breeder.

The price of puppies reflects the care, attention, and costs that a reputable breeder incurs. These breeders do many health checks that will save you money in the long run. Constant monitoring at all hours is required for the first eight weeks, with a great deal of veterinarian bills.

These websites can be good places to begin your search.
Adopt a Pet — http://www.adoptapet.com
Petango — http://www.petango.com
Pet Finder — http://www.petfinder.com

Rescue Organizations and Shelters

When you are considering rescuing a specific breed of dog or puppy, the first place to start your search will be with your local shelter and rescue groups, as well as local breeders.

You can expect to pay an adoption fee to cover the cost of spaying or neutering, which will be only a small percentage of what you would pay a breeder, and will help to support the shelter or rescue facility by defraying their costs.

Initial Vaccinations

If you are purchasing a Jug puppy, you will need to have him properly vaccinated by a veterinarian shortly after you bring him home.

Depending on what kind of treatment the puppy has before you bring him home, you may need to pay for as many as 3 or 4 vaccinations within the first month. You should budget for about $40 (£26) for your puppy's initial vaccinations just to be safe.

Spay/Neuter Surgery

If you do not plan to breed your Jug, it would be wise to have it spayed or neutered. You can have your veterinarian perform the surgery, or if you want to save some money, you might check out the local shelters in your area that offer low-cost spay and neuter clinics.

The cost for spay surgery is generally a little higher than neuter surgery, averaging between $100 and $200 (£65 - £130) at a low-cost clinic versus $50 to $100 (£32.50 - £65) for neuter surgery.

Microchipping

Even if you have your dog licensed, you should still consider having him microchipped as well. A microchip is a small chip that is inserted under your dog's skin that carries a tracking number. If your dog ever gets lost, the chip can be scanned and the number used to find your contact information.

The process for implanting a microchip only takes a few minutes and generally costs less than $50 (£32.50), so it is definitely something you should consider.

Accessories

In addition to buying your Jug, you need to purchase a few accessories to prepare your home for your new pet. Included in this list of accessories are food/water dishes, collar and leash, crate or kennel, toys, and grooming supplies.

The cost for these items will vary greatly depending on the type and quality you choose to buy, but to be safe, you should budget a minimum of $50 (£32.50) and an average of $100 (£65) for these items.

Initial Costs for Jug Dogs		
Cost	**One Dog**	**Two Dogs**
Purchase Price	$200 to $800 (£130 - £500)	$400 to $1600 (£260 - £1000)
Vaccinations	$40 (£26)	$80 (£52)
Spay/Neuter	$50 to $200 (£32.50 - £130)	$100 to $400 (£65 - £260)
Microchipping	$50 (£32.50)	$100 (£65)
Accessories	$50 to $100 (£32.50 - £65)	$100 to $200 (£65 - £130)
Total	$390 to $1190 (£254 - £754)	$780 to $2380 (£507 - £1,507)

Monthly Costs

The monthly costs for a Jug dog include food/treats, veterinary care, license renewal, and other costs.

Given that Jugs are fairly small dogs, they do not eat a great deal of food at any one time. Though your Jug may not eat a lot, it is important that you provide him with a high-quality commercial dog food formulated specifically for small-breed dogs.

Later in this book, you will learn about how small-breed dogs like Jugs have higher energy requirements than large-breed dogs and thus require specially formulated food. You can expect to spend about $25 (£16) on a medium-sized bag of dog food that will last your Jug a month.

In addition to the cost of food, you may want to keep some treats on hand for training – these shouldn't cost you more than $10 (£6.50) per month. This makes your total monthly cost for food and treats about $35 (£22.75).

In order to keep an eye on your Jug's health, especially as he grows up from a puppy, it is a good idea to take him in for a veterinary check-up at least twice per year – about once every six months.

During these check-ups, your vet will perform a physical and oral examination of your Jug and provide recommendations for vaccinations and treatments.

Later in this book, you will read about the vaccinations dogs like Jugs require, but for the most part, your Jug shouldn't require more than one or two a year after his first year.

The average cost of a veterinary check-up is about $35 (£22.75), which averages to around $3 (£1.95) a month.

The cost of vaccinations and medications such as flea/tick preventives and heartworm medications will be about $15 per month extra.

To be safe, the total monthly cost you should set aside for veterinary treatment for your Jug is around $20 (£13).

In addition to the monthly costs for food, veterinary care, and license renewal, there are a few other costs you should budget for on a monthly basis.

These costs may not be necessary each and every month, but it is always a good idea to be prepared. Unexpected costs may include the cost to repair or replace toys and accessories, new collars as your Jug grows, grooming costs, and more.

To be safe, you should budget about $10 (£6.50) per month for these costs.

Monthly Costs for Jug Dogs		
Cost	One Dog	Two Dogs
Food/Treats	$35 (£22.75)	$70 (£45.50)
Veterinary Care	$20 (£13)	$40 (£26)
License Renewal	$2 (£1.30)	$4 (£2.60)
Other Costs	$10 (£6.50)	$20 (£13)
Total	$67 (£40)	$134 (£87)

Are Jugs Easy to Care for?

The answer to this question depends on a variety of factors. If you have never owned a dog before, it may take you some time to get used to the routine of feeding your dog, walking him, and letting him outside – this being the case, you may think that Jugs are a little challenging to care for.

If you are used to the routine of dog ownership, however, you will find that Jugs do not require significantly more care than any other breed. The things to consider in regard to how easy Jugs are to care for include:

- Grooming (short coat, regular brushing required)
- Feeding (two to three meals per day)
- Exercise (moderate requirements, one walk per day)
- Space (small size, can adapt to apartment life)
- Training (can be challenging, consistency required)

All in all, Jugs are relatively easy to care for as long as you do your research and know what to expect before you buy.

Photo Credit: Grandmaster Flash by Emma Fisher

Pros and Cons of Jugs

Before you bring home any new pet, you would be wise to consider the pros and cons. Every pet has its individual advantages and disadvantages, but some will simply be more suitable for you and your family than others.

Pros for Jug Dogs

- Very intelligent breed, generally responds well to firm and consistent training
- Small breed, adaptable to apartments and small houses
- Doesn't necessarily need a yard if given adequate daily exercise
- Generally friendly around people, affectionate with family
- Gets along well with children if properly socialized from a young age
- Makes a great family pet or companion pet
- May get along with other dogs and pets if properly socialized
- Coat is generally short and easy to maintain

Cons for Jug Dogs

- Can be stubborn and may develop "small dog syndrome" if not properly trained
- May be aggressive or jealous toward other dogs if not properly socialized while young
- Prone to several health problems, including obesity and joint problems
- Fairly rare, may be difficult to find at an affordable price
- May become destructive if not properly exercised

Chapter 3 - Purchasing Your Jug

By now you should have a pretty good idea what to expect from keeping a Jug as a pet. After reading the basics about the breed and familiarizing yourself with some of the pros and cons, you may be ready to actually think about buying your Jug.

Photo Credit: Christy Gallois

Where to Buy Your Jug

For many people, the process can seem daunting and confusing. How do you select a breeder? How do you know if you're working with a good breeder? How do you pick a puppy? Are you paying a good price?

When it comes to buying Jugs, your options may be fairly limited because these dogs are still fairly rare. You may be lucky enough to come upon one at your local pet store, but you should consider whether that is really the best place to buy a puppy.

When you buy from a pet store, you cannot be sure where the puppy came from, and you may not have any information about the puppy's parentage. Your best bet is to purchase from a reputable and experienced breeder.

In performing a simple online search, you should be able to find a Jug breeder in your local area or region. You may also be able to ask your veterinarian or local animal shelter for recommendations on where to find breeders.

Below you will find a list of some Jug breeders in both the U.S. and the U.K. from which you can buy puppies:

United States Links:

Greenfield Puppies
http://www.greenfieldpuppies.com/

Sunnyside Puppies
http://www.sunnysidepuppies.com/

Chevromist Kennels
http://www.chevromist.com/jugs/

United Kingdom Links:

Little Rascals
E-mail: info@littlerascalsuk.com
http://littlerascalsuk.com/

Douglas Hall Kennels
http://www.douglashallkennels.co.uk/

Equine Services
http://www.equineservices.co.uk/JackRussellspage.htm

Best Age to Purchase a Puppy

Jug puppies should never be removed from their mother any earlier than 8 weeks of age (at the very earliest), and leaving them until they are 10 to 16 weeks of age is preferred. This gives them time to learn important life skills from the mother dog, including eating solid food and grooming themselves.

Also, a puppy left amongst its litter mates for a longer period of time will learn better socialization skills. Because dogs are descendants of wolves, they are pack animals and prefer company, whether human beings or other dogs. Without social contact, they can become depressed and behave badly.

For the first month of a puppy's life, it will be on a mother's milk-only diet. Once the puppy's teeth begin to appear, it will start to be weaned from mother's milk, and by the age of 8 weeks should be completely weaned and eating just puppy food.

How to Select Your Jug

Take the time to do your research in selecting the right breeder, and then spend some time interacting with all of the puppies available to choose the one that is best suited for you and your family.

You want to be sure that your Jug comes from good quality breeding stock and that the puppies are properly cared for between the time when they are born and when you take your puppy home.

Here is a list of tips for choosing a reputable Jug breeder:

- Compile a list of several breeders in your area and contact them each personally.

- Ask the breeder questions about the Jug breed and about their experience to ascertain whether they are truly professional in their practices or simply a hobby breeder.

- Get as much information from the breeder as you can about their breeding stock, including pedigree information, health history, and more.

- Narrow down your list of breeders based on their answers to your questions – if the breeder doesn't seem knowledgeable about the Jug breed or doesn't have much experience, move on.

- Schedule visits with the few breeders you have narrowed your choices down to.

- Ask to visit the breeding facilities so you can see the parents of the litter, as well as the conditions in which the animals are kept – if the facilities aren't clean, the dogs may not be healthy, so move on to your next option.

- Ask the breeder about the temperament and personalities of the puppy's parents and if they have socialized the puppies.

- You should always have the chance to see the puppy with the mother and its littermates (and if possible, the father). This gives you an opportunity to judge the temperament of one or both parents and to get a better sense of the puppy's eventual size and body conformation.

Good breeders want to know where their puppies are going and what their lives will be like with their new masters. You should be prepared to answer questions about your home and schedule, your family, and any other animals with whom you live.

Don't take this as the breeder being nosy, but rather as an excellent sign of just how much they have invested in the placement of their dogs. If a breeder does NOT ask questions along these lines, be concerned.

Photo Credit: Grandmaster Flash by Emma Fisher

Some people immediately turn into mush when they come face to face with cute little puppies, and still others become very emotional when choosing a puppy, which can lead to being attracted to those who display extremes in behavior.

Take a deep breath, calm yourself, and get back in touch with your common sense. Take the time to choose wisely. People who choose a dog that is not compatible with their energy and lifestyle will inevitably end up with a cascade of troubles.

Below you will find a list of steps to follow when you do visit the puppies to make sure you pick out one that is healthy:

- Take a few minutes to watch the litter of puppies from one side of the room – see how they interact together.

- Look for signs of healthy activity – the puppies shouldn't be hiding in one corner of the room or moving sluggishly.

- Puppies who demonstrate good social skills with their litter mates are much more likely to develop into easy-going, happy adult dogs that play well with others.

- Wait to see if the puppies show an interest in you – Jugs are naturally curious and friendly with people, so the puppies should make their way toward you to smell you.

- Spend a few minutes interacting with each puppy individually to get a feel for his temperament.

- Give the puppy time to sniff you before you pick him up, and gauge his reaction when you do – the puppy should be calm, not frightened of being picked up.

- Check the puppy for obvious signs of illness – discharge from the nose or mouth, cloudy eyes, palpable lumps or bumps.

- Play with the puppies to see how they react to you and see which one you feel a connection with.

- Always ask if a Jug puppy you are interested in has displayed any signs of aggression or fear, because if this is happening at such an early age, you may experience behavioral troubles as the puppy becomes older.

Check Puppy's Health

Ask to see veterinarian reports to satisfy yourself that the puppy is as healthy as possible, and then once you make your decision to share your life with a particular puppy, make an appointment with your own veterinarian for a complete examination.

Before making your final pick of the litter, check for general signs of good health, including the following:

1. Breathing: will be quiet, without coughing or sneezing, and there will be no crusting or discharge around their nostrils.
2. Body: will look round and well-fed, with an obvious layer of fat over their rib cage.
3. Coat: will be soft with no dandruff or bald spots.
4. Energy: a well-rested puppy should be alert and energetic.
5. Hearing: a puppy should react if you clap your hands behind their head.
6. Genitals: no discharge visible in or around their genital or anal region.
7. Mobility: they will walk and run normally without wobbling, limping, or seeming to be stiff or sore.
8. Vision: bright, clear eyes with no crust or discharge.

What the Breeder Should Provide to You

In most cases, breeders allow potential owners to come visit the puppies before they are ready to go home.

The standard procedure is to put down a deposit on the puppy to claim it – you will then return for the puppy when he has been weaned and is ready to leave.

The breeder should supply all of the following to you:

- You should receive a contract of sale that details the responsibilities of both parties in the adoption of the dog.

The document should also explain how the puppy's registration papers will be transferred to you.

- There should be a written document that offers advice on feeding, training, and exercise, as well as necessary health procedures like worming and vaccinations.

- Make sure that you receive copies of all health records for the puppy (and parents), in particular what vaccinations the dog has received and the required schedule for booster shots. Good breeders also offer full disclosure of any potential genetic conditions associated with the breed and are willing to discuss any testing that has been done to screen for these issues.

- You should also receive a guarantee of the puppy's health at the time of adoption, which you will likely be asked to confirm, for the safety of both parties, by taking the animal to a vet for evaluation. There should also be a detailed explanation of recompense in the event that a health condition does arise within a set period of time.

Puppy-proofing Your Home

If you have never lived with a puppy, or it has been a long time since you've shared your home with one, you may not realize or remember what a force of nature a growing dog can really be!

Take the attitude that you are bringing home a baby on four legs. Just as you would make sure that all the hazards have been removed from the house for an infant or toddler, do the same for your Jug puppy. I promise, he will explore every nook and cranny, and he'll try to chew on every "discovery" he unearths.

- Keep all loose articles and small objects off the floor – place them on shelves or in cabinets where your puppy can't reach them.

- Secure cabinets and cupboards – especially those that contain toxic materials like cleaning products – so your puppy can't open them.

- Wrap phone wires and electric cords to keep your puppy from chewing on them and hurting himself.

- Consider wrapping your table legs to keep your puppy from chewing them.

- Block access to dangerous areas inside and outside your home – make sure your fence locks securely and block off stairs and doorways to rooms you don't want your puppy to have access to.

Household and Garden Plants

A wide variety of household and garden plants present a toxic risk to dogs. You may have heard about the dangers of apricot and peach pits, but what about spinach and tomato vines? The American Society for the Prevention of Cruelty to Animals has created a large reference list of plants that runs to several pages.

http://www.aspca.org/pet-care/animal-poison-control/toxic-and-non-toxic-plants

I strongly recommend you go through the list and remove any plants from your home that might make your puppy sick. Remember, your new baby will chew on everything!

Bringing Your Puppy Home

Purchase an appropriate travel crate to bring your Jug puppy home. A plastic crate with a fastening wire door and a carry handle is your best option. Since your puppy will be very small, you can start with a unit measuring 24" x 16.5" x 15" / 60.96 cm x 41.91 cm x 38.1 cm. That size will accommodate a dog in a weight range of 10 lbs to 20 lbs / 4.53 kg 9.07 kg. Expect to pay around $30 / £17.84.

Put a couple of puppy-safe chew toys and an article of clothing you've worn recently in the crate. This will help the puppy to get to "know" you and will make the crate seem more like a "den" or safe haven. Place the puppy inside the crate and fasten the seatbelt over the crate to keep it secure on the drive home.

Make sure that the puppy has not eaten recently and has taken care of its "business" before it goes in the crate. Discuss this in advance with the kennel owner and schedule a pick-up time in between feedings. Be prepared. The little dog will whine and cry, especially if the drive is long.

Photo Credit: Frank by Tim Webb

If you have to drive a considerable distance, some breeders suggest mildly sedating the puppy. If you are not comfortable with this idea, take someone with you who can sit with the dog and comfort it on the way home.

Don't take more than one other person with you, however, and leave the kids at home. Having too many people in the car for the transition from kennel to new home will stress and confuse the little dog. You want the trip to be a calm, quiet, and positive experience for your new Jug.

When you arrive home, let the puppy have a little time outside to relieve itself. Start reinforcing good elimination habits immediately and praise the puppy. Dogs like to please, so associate going outside with being a "good dog."

The Jug will naturally be nervous and will miss its familiar surroundings in the beginning, so try to stick to the feeding schedule used at the kennel, and use the same kind of food if possible. Put the puppy in its designated area in the house and let it explore, making sure the dog isn't isolated and can see you.

Don't pick the puppy up every time it cries. You'll be reinforcing that behavior and the next thing you know, you'll be spending all your time holding the dog. Jugs, no matter how young, are not above "working" their humans.

Continue to give the puppy used pieces of clothing with your scent, play a radio softly in the room, and at night put a well-wrapped, warm hot water bottle in the crate.

Jugs and Children

If you have children, slowly introduce the puppy to them. This is not for the sake of the kids, but for the benefit of the puppy!

Explain to your children, especially if they are very young, that the dog is away from its mother and the only home it has known for the first time and is scared.

Limit the amount of playtime with the puppy and how much it is handled during the first days. Emphasize quiet, gentle, "getting to know each other" time with your children. In just a matter of days, the puppy will be playing with them joyfully.

Be sure that your children know how to safely handle and carry the puppy. Monitor the first few interactions. If your child has never been around a dog and seems slightly afraid, spend time with them and help them to get to know the puppy for the safety and comfort of all concerned.

Introductions With Other Pets

Keep other pets away from your puppy for the first few days. Let the puppy smell the other pet's bedding (and vice versa) or allow sniffing under the closed bathroom door — a tried and true method of negotiating such meetings.

Carefully supervise the first face-to-face meeting. Other dogs should be on leashes, and cats should be held until they are comfortable with even the sight of the new dog. Gradually extend the period of exposure, and calmly separate the animals at the first sign of aggression.

Pets take their emotional cues from us. You must set the tone for first introductions. Remain calm. Don't raise your voice. Praise good behavior. Do nothing to "punish" bad behavior beyond separating the animals. Keep the meetings short and positive, without stress or trauma.

Helping Your Puppy Settle in

• Before you bring your puppy home, establish rules with your children regarding the handling and care of the puppy.

• Plan a routine for when you will walk and feed your puppy – having a set routine will make things easier for you both.

• Set up a special area of the house with your puppy's crate along with his food/water bowl and toys – this area should be in a place that is quiet but easily accessible.

• When you get your puppy home, let him outside immediately – choose a particular portion of the yard where you want him to do his business and maintain consistency in potty training.

• Engage your new puppy in brief periods of playtime throughout the day for the first few days, but give him plenty of rest – it will take time for him to adjust.

• Block off rooms where you do not want your puppy to go – it is a good idea to limit your puppy's range to only the room you are in until he is potty trained.

• Introduce your puppy to new experiences slowly – do not overwhelm him by inviting all of your friends over to meet him on the first day.

Common Mistakes to Avoid

Never pick your puppy up if they are showing fear or aggression toward an object, another dog, or person, because this will be rewarding them for unbalanced behavior.

If they are doing something you do not want them to continue, your puppy needs to be gently corrected by you with firm and calm energy, so that they learn not to react with fear or aggression.

Don't play the "hand" game, where you slide the puppy across the floor with your hands, because it's amusing for humans to see a little ball of fur scrambling to collect themselves and run back across the floor for another go. This sort of "game" will teach your puppy to disrespect you as its leader in two different ways — first, because this "game" teaches them that humans are play toys, and secondly, this type of "game" teaches the puppy that humans are a source of excitement.

Photo Credit: Grandmaster Flash by Emma Fisher

When your Jug puppy is teething, they will naturally want to chew on everything within reach, and this will include you. As cute as you might think it is when they are young puppies, this is not an acceptable behavior, and you need to gently, but firmly, discourage the habit, just like a mother dog does to her puppies when they need to be weaned.

Always praise your puppy when they stop inappropriate behavior, as this is the beginning of teaching them to understand rules and boundaries. Often we humans are quick to discipline puppies or dogs for inappropriate behavior, but we forget to praise them for their good behavior.

Don't treat your Jug like a small, furry human. When people try to turn them into small, furry people, this can cause them much stress and confusion that could lead to behavioral problems.

A well-behaved Jug thrives on rules and boundaries, and when they understand that there is no question you are their leader and they are your follower, they will live a contented, happy, and stress-free life.

Dogs are a different species with different rules; for example, they do not naturally cuddle and therefore they need to learn to be stroked and cuddled by humans. Therefore, be careful when approaching a dog for the first time and being overly expressive with your hands. The safest areas to touch are the back and chest — avoid patting on the head and touching the ears.

Photo Credit: Jimtography

Many people will assume that a dog that is yawning is tired —
this is often a misinterpretation, and instead it is signaling your
dog is uncomfortable and nervous about a situation.

Be careful when staring at dogs, because this is one of the ways
in which they threaten each other. This body language can make
them feel distinctly uneasy.

What Can I Do to Make My Jug Love Me?

From the moment you bring your Jug dog home, every minute
you spend with him is an opportunity to bond. The earlier you
start working with your dog, the more quickly that bond will
grow and the closer you and your Jug will become.

While simply spending time with your Jug will encourage the
growth of that bond, there are a few things you can do to
purposefully build your bond with your dog. Some of these
things include:

- Taking your Jug for daily walks during which you
  frequently stop to pet and talk to your dog.

- Engaging your Jug in games like tug of war, fetch, and
  hide-and-seek to encourage interaction.

- Interact with your dog through daily training sessions –
  teach your dog to pay attention when you say his name.

- Be calm and consistent when training your dog – always
  use positive reinforcement rather than punishment.

- Spend as much time with your dog as possible, even if it
  means simply keeping the dog in the room with you
  while you cook dinner or pay bills.

Chapter 4 - Caring for Your Jug

In order to provide your Jug with the best care possible, you need to understand his habitat requirements, nutritional needs, and grooming requirements.

Photo Credit: Frank by Tim Webb

Habitat Requirements

Unlike many pets, your Jug doesn't require a "habitat" in the form of a cage. There are, however, certain things you need to do in order to make your home Jug-friendly. Some of the basic things you are going to need for your Jug may include the following:

Food and water bowls
A crate or kennel
A dog bed or soft blanket
Plenty of dog toys
Space to run and play

Setting up Your Jug's Area

Before you bring your Jug home, you should set aside a certain area in the house as his little zone. This is where you should keep your Jug's crate, along with his food and water dishes and toys.

The idea behind this is to provide your Jug with a little place to call his own – a place where he can come to relax and take a nap if he wants to. Ideally, your Jug should come to view his crate as simply a place to sleep and not a form of punishment.

The ideal placement for this area is in a room of the house where your dog will not feel isolated. It shouldn't be in the busiest part of the house either, however.

Once you establish this place, do not move it often – the idea is to give your dog a place where he feels secure, and that might not happen if you rearrange things too often.

Where Will Your Jug Sleep?

I admit that I'm as guilty as anyone of letting my dogs sleep with me, but crate training a puppy from an early age will provide you both with better peace of mind in the long run.

A dog trained to sleep in a crate has a "den" of his own and will feel much safer and be more content when you're not at home. Also, dogs won't soil the area where they sleep, so getting in a crate routine from day one will help to facilitate housetraining.

You have two choices in crate styles: plastic portable units like those used to transport your pet to the vet, and a wire crate. Either should be large enough for the puppy to stand up, turn around, and lie down comfortably. Good ventilation is also essential. For this reason, I prefer a wire crate outfitted with comfortable padding.

Photo Credit: Sergei by Mercedes Clark-Smith

You can buy an adult-sized crate for a puppy; just make sure you give the little dog a cardboard box tucked away in the back corner, so he has a cozy space to snuggle into.

In addition to the crate, which you will use when you are away and at night, you can also have one or more puppy/dog beds in the home for those moments when your little Jug wants a nap.

That's one of the funniest things about puppies. They go at full speed until they don't, and then they collapse into an adorable, snoring pile.

For a breed like the Jug, you'll want a wire crate that is 30" x 19" x 22" / 76.2 cm x 48.26 cm x 55.88 cm, which should retail for less than $50 / £29.73. Expect to spend an additional $25 / £14.87 on a good quality crate pad.

Exercising Your Jug

Being a cross between the Pug and the Jack Russell Terrier, Jugs are a fairly active breed of dog. This being the case, you need to provide them with plenty of daily exercise – at least 30 minutes once a day.

If you have a fenced yard where your dog can run around, that is great, but it shouldn't be viewed as a substitute for taking your dog on a walk at least once a day.

If you do not take your Jug for walks often enough, he is more likely to develop "small dog syndrome." This is especially common in small breed dogs like Pugs and Jack Russell Terriers – they eventually become very dominant and stubborn and may be less likely to respond to commands.

Dogs that don't get enough exercise are also more likely to develop problem behaviors like chewing, digging, and barking.

Some tips for giving your Jug extra exercise include:

- Play a game of tug-of-war with your dog in the house.

- Engage your dog in a game of hide-and-seek.

- Play fetch with your dog outside in the back yard.

- Take your Jug to the dog park to play with other dogs.

Playtime is important, especially for a dog's natural desire to chase. Try channeling this instinct with toys and games. If a dog has no stimulation and has nothing to chase, they can start to chase their own tail, which can lead to problems.

Toys can be used to simulate the dog's natural desire to hunt. For example, when they catch a toy, they will often shake it and bury their teeth into it, simulating the killing of their prey.

Allow your dog to fulfill a natural desire to chew. This comes from historically catching their prey and then chewing the carcass. Providing chews or bones can prevent your dog from destroying your home.

Playing with your dog is not only a great way of getting them to use up their energy, but it is also a great way of bonding with them as they have fun. Dogs love to chase and catch balls; just make sure that the ball is too large to be swallowed.

When picking out toys for your Jug regardless of his age, don't get anything soft and "shred-able." Jugs can be regular engines of destruction!

I recommend small chew toys like Nylabones that can withstand the abuse. You can buy items made out of this tough material in the $1 - $5 / £0.59 - £2.97 range.

Deer antlers are wonderful toys for Jugs. Most love them. They do not smell, are all-natural, and do not stain or splinter. I recommend the antlers that are not split, as the split ones do not last as long.

Never give your dog rawhide, cow hooves, or pig's ears. The rawhide and pig's ears become soft and present choking hazards, while the cow hooves can splinter and puncture the cheek or palate.

Avoid soft rubber toys that can be chewed into pieces and swallowed. Opt for rope toys instead. Don't buy anything with a squeaker or any other part that presents a choking hazard.

Standard Leash or Retractable?

For the most part, the decision to buy a standard, fixed-length leash or a retractable lead is up to you. Do bear in mind that some facilities like groomers, vet clinics, and dog daycares ask that you not bring your animal in on a retractable lead, as the long line represents a trip and fall hazard.

Fixed length leashes can cost as little as $5 / £2.97, while retractable leads are typically less than $15 / £8.91.

Regardless of the kind of lead you choose, your dog will have to get used to responding to your control of the leash.

Some Tips on Walking Your Dog

Because walks and going out are things that dogs enjoy, and because your pet will want to please you, you can instill some good behaviors on command around the whole process. Teach your dog the "sit" command by using the word and making a downward pointing motion with your finger or the palm of your hand.

Reward the dog with a treat each time he performs correctly. Then pair the sit command with the pleasure of a walk by refusing to attach the lead to the harness until your pet sits. Make attaching the leash and saying, "Okay, let's go!" be the reward.

Any time the dog tries to pull you or jerk at the leash, stop the walk, pick up the dog, and start over with the sit command. Praise and reward the dog for walking properly at the end of the lead and for stopping when you stop. The more than you can reinforce the walk as a shared activity, the quieter and more calm your dog will be.

Your dog's main sense is scent, which is why when you take them for a walk they spend a lot of time sniffing everything. They gather an amazing amount of information, such as being able to determine which dogs were recently in the area, their gender, their current health, and age.

When two dogs meet, they are likely to go up to each other and sniff near each other's jaw and then around the rear-end area.

Have you ever visited a friend and their dog has come up to you and sniffed your groin area? This may have caused some embarrassment, but this is simply a dog's way of learning about you by picking up scents.

Puppy Nutrition

Dogs require a graduated program of nutrition as they age. Puppies of four months or less should receive four small meals a day. From age four to eight months, switch to three meals per day, and then twice daily feedings at eight months and older.

Put your puppy's food down for approximately 10-20 minutes, and then take it back up again. Do not use the practice of "free feeding," which is leaving dry food out for the dog at all times.

Use only a high-quality, premium, dry puppy food, preferably whatever the dog was used to eating at the kennel. Switching foods can lead to gastrointestinal upset, so try to maintain the dog's existing routine in so much as it is possible to do so.

Always read the label on any food you purchase to ensure that the first items listed are meat, fishmeal, or whole grains. You do not want to use a food that contains large amounts of cornmeal or meat byproducts. These "filler foods" are low in nutritional value and increase the amount of waste the dog will produce per day, as well as adding to flatulence problems.

Wet foods can cause digestive issues with Jug puppies and may not have the correct nutritional balance for your growing dog. Wet foods are also more difficult to measure, so the chances are much greater that the puppy will be over or under fed.

Portion control is extremely important with this breed. Measure the dry food you offer your dog, and use only the recommended portion based on the puppy's weight.

Use food and water dishes that can't be tipped over. Stainless steel bowls are easier to keep clean and can be purchased as part of a unit that will slightly elevate the feeding surface. Even though your puppy may not be "tall" enough for that option just yet, he can grow into it, so you won't have to replace his dishes in the future.

Feeders with stainless steel bowls for both food and water are typically available for less than $25 / £14.87. Stainless steel is best because they are easy to clean, and they do not harbor bacteria like plastic or ceramic dishes can.

Nutritional Needs

The first thing you need to realize when it comes to feeding your Jug dog is that different breeds of dogs have different feeding requirements. That isn't to say that one breed needs a different set of nutrients than another – nutritional needs simply vary depending on the size of the dog.

Because Jugs are a small breed of dog, they have higher energy requirements than larger breeds and must be fed certain types of food.

Dogs, like all animals, require a balanced diet made up of carbohydrates, protein, and fat. It is important that you understand, however, that the ideal ratio of these nutrients is different for dogs than it is for other animals like cats, or even humans.

Below you will find a brief explanation of why each of these nutrients is essential for your Jug:

Protein – You have probably heard that proteins are the building blocks of healthy tissues and organs, so you can see why they are such an important part of a Jug's diet.

The best protein sources for your dog include chicken, beef, turkey, lamb, fish, and eggs – protein can also be found in certain vegetables and soy, but these are not the best sources of protein for your dog.

Fats – Fats provide your dog with a highly concentrated source of energy – this is especially important for small breed dogs like Jugs, because they burn energy at a higher rate than large-breed dogs.

Fats are also essential because they help your dog's body to absorb fat-soluble vitamins, and they play a role in insulating his organs.

Some of the most important essential fatty acids for dogs include linoleic acid, omega-3 fatty acid, and omega-6 fatty acid.

Carbohydrates – These nutrients provide energy for your dog's tissues, and they also provide fiber, which is essential for digestive health. Some of the best sources of fiber for your dog include beet pulp and rice. It is important to note that while your dog's diet should contain carbohydrates, fats and protein are most important.

Photo Credit: John McQuillan

Water – Another important nutrient your Jug needs is water. You should plan to provide your Jug with unlimited access to fresh water on a daily basis. Have at least one large bowl of fresh water placed somewhere your Jug can easily access it, and refill the bowl as needed throughout the day.

Water is also an important element of your dog's food – most commercial dry foods contain as much as 10% water, and wet foods contain even more.

Other Nutrients – In addition to these basic nutrients, your dog also requires various vitamins and minerals to remain healthy. Vitamins are the catalysts your dog's body needs for enzyme reactions, and because most vitamins can't be synthesized, your dog needs to get them through his diet.

The same is true for minerals – they cannot be synthesized by the body, but they are essential for maintaining fluid balance, and they play a role in many essential metabolic reactions in the body.

The BARF Diet

Raw feeding advocates believe that the ideal diet for their dog is one that would be very similar to what a dog living in the wild would have access to, and these canine guardians are often opposed to feeding their dog any sort of commercially manufactured pet foods.

On the other hand, those opposed to feeding their dogs a raw or Biologically Appropriate Raw Food (BARF) diet believe that the risks associated with food-borne illnesses during the handling and feeding of raw meats outweigh the purported benefits.

Raw meats purchased at your local grocery store contain a much higher level of acceptable bacteria than raw food produced for dogs, because the meat purchased for human consumption is meant to be cooked, which will kill any bacteria.

This means that canine guardians feeding their dogs a raw food diet can be quite certain that commercially prepared raw foods sold in pet stores will be safer than raw meats purchased in grocery stores.

Many guardians of high energy, working breed dogs will agree that their dogs thrive on a raw or BARF diet and strongly believe that the potential benefits of feeding a dog a raw food diet are many, including:

- Healthy, shiny coats
- Decreased shedding
- Fewer allergy problems
- Healthier skin
- Cleaner teeth
- Fresher breath
- Higher energy levels
- Improved digestion
- Smaller stools
- Strengthened immune system
- Increased mobility in arthritic pets
- General increase or improvement in overall health

All dogs, whether working breed or lap dogs, are amazing athletes in their own right, therefore every dog deserves to be fed the best food available.

A raw diet is a direct evolution of what dogs ate before they became our domesticated pets and we turned toward commercially prepared, easy-to-serve dry dog food that required no special storage or preparation.

The Dehydrated Diet

Dehydrated dog food comes in both raw and cooked forms, and these foods are usually air-dried to reduce moisture to the level where bacterial growth is inhibited.

The appearance of dehydrated dog food is very similar to dry kibble, and the typical feeding methods include adding warm water before serving, which makes this type of diet both healthy for our dogs and convenient for us to serve.

Dehydrated recipes are made from minimally processed fresh whole foods to create a healthy and nutritionally balanced meal that will meet or exceed the dietary requirements for healthy canines.

Dehydrating removes only the moisture from the fresh ingredients, which usually means that because the food has not already been cooked at a high temperature, more of the overall nutrition is retained.

A dehydrated diet is a convenient way to feed your dog a nutritious diet, because all you have to do is add warm water and wait five minutes while the food re-hydrates so your Jug can enjoy a warm meal.

How Much to Feed

Now that you understand the basics of what your dog needs nutritionally, you may be wondering just how much food you should be giving him on a daily basis. A Jug's energy needs vary depending on his age and activity level.

When your Jug is a puppy, he should be getting about 4 small meals per day to provide his body with a constant source of energy to sustain growth. As your Jug gets older, his metabolism will slow down, and he may only need two feedings per day.

Age	Daily Feedings	Amount of Food
3 to 6 months	3 to 4	1/3 cup
6 to 12 months	2 to 3	3/4 cup
1 to 8 years	2	1/2 cup
8+ years	2	1/3 cup

Choosing a Dog Food

When it comes to choosing the right food for your Jug, it can be a difficult decision – there are so many options to choose from.

Next you will find some tips to help you choose a commercial dog food formula that will provide for your Jug's nutritional and energy needs:

•   The first ingredient on the list should be a whole meat source – chicken, not chicken meal (and certainly not some other product like corn or wheat).

•   Select a formula that is designed for small breed dogs, because the pieces will be smaller and easier for your Jug to eat.

•   Compare the fat content of various formulas – small breeds like Jugs require more fat for energy than large breed dogs.

•   Look for easily digestible sources of carbohydrate on the ingredients list – things like cooked rice, oats and barley.

•   Consider avoiding common allergens in dog foods like wheat and corn.

•   Look for an AAFCO statement of nutritional adequacy on the package – this states that the food meets certain nutritional requirements.

•   Check to be sure that the food contains at least 18% (dry matter) protein for adult dogs and 22% for puppies and pregnant/lactating females.

•   Look for a food that provides at least 5% (dry matter) fat for adult dogs and 8% for puppies and pregnant/lactating females.

Most dog food packages list the amounts of specific nutrients in the Guaranteed Analysis. Unfortunately, most of these list foods expressed in an "as fed" basis, which can be misleading – a more accurate measurement is dry matter.

To find the dry matter content of a food, look at the moisture content of the food and subtract that from 100%.

For example, a food that has 10% moisture has 90% dry matter. Then, divide the "as fed" amount of each nutrient by that 90% to find the dry matter content of each nutrient.

Ex: If you have a product with 90% dry matter and 20% protein "as fed," you would divide 20% by 90% to find the dry matter content – 22%.

What Should I Never Feed my Jug?

There is not a dog owner on earth who can say that he never fed his dog scraps from the table or dropped him a "treat" once in a while.

It is important to realize, however, that there are some foods that you may not know are harmful for dogs. Below you will find a list of foods that you should never feed your Jug:

Alcohol
Apple seeds
Avocado
Cherry pits
Candy

Chocolate
Coffee
Garlic
Grapes
Gum
Hops
Macadamia nuts
Mushroom
Mustard seeds
Onions
Peach pits
Potato stems
Raisins
Rhubarb leaves
Salt
Tea
Tomato leaves
Walnuts
Xylitol
Yeast

If you allow your puppy to chew on a bone, monitor the dog closely. Use only small knuckle or joint bones. Remove the item at the first sign of splintering. Most owners prefer commercial chew toys that are rated "puppy safe."

Grooming

Do not allow yourself to get caught in the "my dog doesn't like it" trap, which is an excuse many owners will use to avoid regular grooming sessions. When you allow your dog to dictate whether they will permit a grooming session, you are setting a dangerous precedent.

Once you have bonded with your dog, they love to be tickled, rubbed, and scratched in certain favorite places. This is why grooming is a great source of pleasure and a way to bond with your pet.

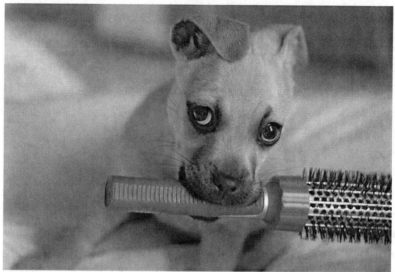

Photo Credit: Grandmaster Flash by Emma Fisher

For the most part, grooming your Jug means brushing it once a week with a slicker brush costing less than $10 / £5.94. Since this will be time spent with you, likely in your lap, your Jug will be completely onboard with the process!

This is also an excellent opportunity to examine your dog's skin for any growths, lumps, bumps, or wounds and to have a good look at his ears, eyes, and mouth.

Jugs are not terribly difficult to groom, though the length and texture of their coats may vary slightly depending on breeding.

For the most part, you should only need to brush your Jug's coat once or twice a week and bathe him every few months.

Avoid over-bathing your dog, because it could dry out and irritate his skin. You should only plan to bathe your Jug when he is being groomed, or when he really needs to be bathed.

Follow the tips below to groom your Jug appropriately:

1.) Place your Jug on a flat surface at waist-height – a counter or table will do.

2.) Go over your Jug's coat by hand to see if there are any mats in his fur – if there are, carefully work them free or cut them out with a small pair of sharp scissors.

3.) Use a fine-toothed comb to remove dead hairs from your Jug's coat – start at the base of the neck and work down the back, then move on to the legs and belly.

4.) Go over your dog's coat with a slicker brush to remove fur from the undercoat – this will help prevent shedding.

5.) Rub down your Jug with a velvet cloth to give his coat a nice sheen – this is a common practice in grooming Pugs and, depending on the texture of your Jug's coat, it should work on him as well.

How to Bathe Your Jug

The earlier you start bathing your Jug, the easier it is going to be – if your Jug gets used to it as a puppy, then he will be less difficult to handle later. Follow the tips below to bathe your Jug:

1.) Fill a bathtub with several inches of warm water – make sure it is not too hot.

2.) Place your Jug in the tub and wet down his coat.

3.) Apply a dollop of dog shampoo to your hands and work it into your Jug's coat, starting at the base of his neck.

4.) Work the shampoo into your dog's back and down his legs and tail.

5.)   Rinse your dog well, making sure to get rid of all the soap.

6.)   Towel dry your jug to remove as much moisture as possible.

7.)   If desired, use a hair dryer on the cool setting to dry your Jug's coat the rest of the way.

It is very important that you avoid getting water in your Jug's ears and eyes. If your Jug's ears get wet, dry them carefully with a cotton ball to prevent infection.

Fleas and Ticks

If you are going to have a dog for a pet, the time will come when you find a flea on your pet. This is not the dog's fault, nor is it the end of the world. You want to deal with the problem immediately, but in the short term, the flea is far happier on the dog than it would be on you.

Never treat a puppy of less than 12 weeks of age with a commercial flea product, and be extremely careful of using these items on adult dogs as well. Most of the major brand products contain pyrethrum, which has been responsible for adverse reactions in small dogs to the point of being fatal. Others have recovered, but suffered life-long neurological damage.

The very best thing you can do to get rid of fleas is to give your dog a bath in warm water using a standard canine shampoo. Comb the animal's fur with a fine-toothed flea comb. Any live fleas that you collect in the comb will die when you submerge the comb in hot soapy water.

Wash all of the dog's bedding and any soft materials with which he has come in contact in hot water. Look for any accumulations of "flea dirt," which is actually excreted blood from adult fleas.

Continue washing the bedding and other surfaces daily for at least a week. You are trying to remove any remaining eggs, so that no new fleas hatch out.

If you find a tick on your dog, you can remove the blood-sucking parasite by first coating it with a thick layer of petroleum jelly.

Leave this on for up to 5 minutes. The jelly clogs the spiracles through which the tick breathes and causes its jaws to release. You can then simply pluck the tick off with a pair of tweezers with a straight motion. Never just jerk a tick off a dog. The head of the creature will be left behind and will continue to burrow into the skin, making a painful sore.

Other Care Tips

In addition to bathing and grooming your Jug, there are a few other things you need to do to care for him. On a weekly basis, ideally when you brush him, you should check your Jug's ears to make sure they are clean.

If your Jug's ears have a waxy discharge or a foul odor, it could be a sign of infection so take him to the vet as soon as possible. If you need to clean your dog's ears, use a dog ear cleaning solution and a clean cotton ball.

Every few weeks, you will need to trim your Jug's toenails to keep them from getting too long. The more time your dog spends outside, the more worn down they will naturally be, but you may still need to trim them sometimes.

Trimming a dog's nails can be tricky, so you may want to have a professional groomer or veterinarian show you how to do it before you try it for the first time.

A Jug's nail contains a quick, the blood vessel that supplies blood to the nail – if you cut the nail too short you could sever the quick, which will result in pain for your dog and profuse bleeding. Trim only as much of the nail as you need to without cutting into the quick.

Photo Credit: Grandmaster Flash by Emma Fisher

Always use a nail trimmer designed for use with dogs. I prefer the kind with plier grips, as they are easier to handle and are inexpensive, selling for under $20 / £11.88

I really recommend using one of the "Dremel" type hand-held grinders for nails. It is basically just a rotating emery wheel and presents no issues with pinching their nails as with a "chopper" type nail clipper. Only use a slow speed Dremel, such as Model 7300-PT Pet Nail Grooming Tool (approx. $40/£20).

Chapter 5 - Training Your Jug

Training starts from the minute you bring your Jug home. You may not realize it, but everything you do teaches your Jug puppy how to act. Many dog owners make the mistake of giving their puppy free reign for the first few weeks, and then they are surprised when it comes time for training and the puppy has already developed hard-to-break habits.

If you want to raise a well-trained and obedient Jug, you should start your training early by rewarding your puppy for doing the things you want him to do and discouraging him from unwanted behaviors.

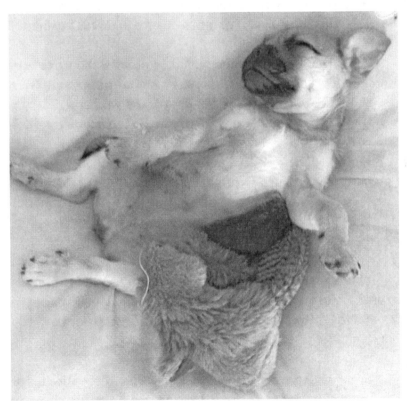

Photo Credit: Sergei by Mercedes Clark-Smith

Housetraining Guide

If you are buying your Jug as a puppy, the first thing you have to worry about is housetraining. Many dog owners mistakenly assume that housetraining is a long and drawn-out process. If you do it correctly, however, it can actually be very simple, and your puppy could be housetrained in as little as 14 days.

1.) Select a certain portion of the yard where you want your dog to do his business – this will help reduce the amount you have to clean up after your dog and will clarify your expectations when you take your dog out.

2.) As soon as you bring your puppy home, take him outside to the designated area and give him a chance to do his business.

3.) When you take your dog outside, you may choose to use a command like "go potty" or "go pee," so your puppy will learn to associate the command with that area of the yard and, subsequently, learn what you want him to do when you say it.

4.) Limit your puppy's reign in the house to whatever room you are in – this will help to prevent accidents.

5.) Take your puppy outside once every hour or so and give him a chance to do his business.

6.) When your puppy does his business in the designated area, praise him excitedly and offer him a treat – if your puppy learns that this behavior pleases you, he will be more apt to repeat it in the future.

7.) Always take your puppy outside within thirty minutes of a meal and just before bed time – these are the times when your puppy is most likely to need to "go."

8.)   Keep your puppy in the crate overnight and do not leave food or water in the crate – this will only increase the likelihood of an accident.

9.)   Make sure the crate is only large enough for your puppy to stand up, turn around and lie down – dogs have a natural aversion to soiling their beds, so if there isn't a lot of extra space, it will dissuade your puppy from having an accident in it.

10.)   Do not leave your puppy in the crate for more than 3 or 4 hours at a time – as your puppy gets older, he will develop the ability to control his bladder over longer periods of time.

11.)   Take your puppy out of the crate and outside as soon as you wake up in the morning.

From your puppy's point of view, yelling or screaming when they make a potty mistake is unstable energy being displayed by the person who is supposed to be their leader, and this type of behavior will only teach your puppy to fear and disrespect you.

Never punish a dog for having an accident. They cannot relate the punishment to the incident. If you catch them in the act you can say "bad dog," but don't go on and on about it. Clean up the accident using an enzymatic cleaner to eliminate the odor and return to the dog's normal routine.

Nature's Miracle Stain and Odor Removal is excellent for these kinds of incidents and is very affordable at $5 / £2.97 per 32 ounce / 0.9 liter bottle.

Go to http://www.removeurineodors.com and order some "SUN" and/or "Max Enzyme" – these products contain professional-strength odor neutralizers and urine digesters that bind to and completely absorb and eliminate odors on any type of surface.

Marking Territory

Both intact male and female dogs will mark territory by urinating. This is most often an outdoor behavior, but can happen inside if a new dog is introduced to the household.

Again, use an enzymatic cleaner to remove the odor so the dog will not be attracted to use the same spot again. Since this behavior is most often seen in intact males displaying dominance, the obvious solution is to have the dog neutered.

If this is not possible, and the behavior continues, it may be necessary to separate the animals or to work with a trainer to resolve dominance issues in your little "pack." Marking territory is not a consequence of poor housetraining, and the behavior can be seen in dogs that would otherwise never go in the house.

If you are consistent in taking your puppy outside frequently and in rewarding him for good behavior (doing his business in the designated area), you should have no trouble at all with housetraining.

Dog Whispering

Many people can be confused when they need professional help with their dog, because for many years, if you needed help with your dog, you contacted a "dog trainer" or took your dog to "puppy classes" where your dog would learn how to sit or stay.

The difference between a dog trainer and a dog whisperer would be that a "dog trainer" teaches a dog how to perform certain tasks, and a "dog whisperer" alleviates behavior problems by teaching humans what they need to do to keep their particular dog happy.

Often, depending on how soon the guardian has sought help, this can mean that the dog in question has developed some pretty serious issues, such as aggressive barking, lunging, biting, or attacking other dogs, pets, or people.

Dog whispering is often an emotional roller coaster ride for the humans involved that unveils many truths when they finally realize that it has been their actions (or inactions) that have likely caused the unbalanced behavior that their dog is now displaying.

Once solutions are provided, the relief for both dog and human can be quite cathartic when they realize that with the correct direction, they can indeed live a happy life with their dog.

All specific methods of training, such as "clicker training," fall outside of what every dog needs to be happy, because training your dog to respond to a clicker, which you can easily do on your own, and then letting them sleep in your bed, eat from your plate, and any other multitude of things humans allow, are what makes the dog unbalanced and causes behavior problems.

I always say to people, don't wait until you have a severe problem before getting some dog whispering or professional help of some sort, because "With the proper training, Man can learn to be dog's best friend."

Rewarding Unwanted Behavior

It is very important to recognize that any attention paid to an out-of-control, adolescent puppy, even negative attention, is likely to be exciting and rewarding for your Jug puppy.

Chasing after a puppy when they have taken something they shouldn't have, picking them up when barking or showing aggression, pushing them off when they jump on other people, or yelling when they refuse to come when called, are all forms of attention that can actually be rewarding for most puppies.

It will be your responsibility to provide structure for your puppy, which will include finding acceptable and safe ways to allow your puppy to vent their energy without being destructive or harmful to others.

The worst thing you can do when training your Jug is to yell at him or use punishment. Positive reinforcement training methods – that is, rewarding your dog for good behavior – are infinitely more effective than negative reinforcement – training by punishment.

It is important when training your Jug that you do not allow yourself to get frustrated. If you feel yourself starting to get angry, take a break and come back to the training session later.

Why is punishment-based training so bad? Think about it this way – your dog should listen to you because he wants to please you, right?

If you train your dog using punishment, he could become fearful of you, and that could put a damper on your relationship with him. Do your dog and yourself a favor by using positive reinforcement.

Teaching Basic Commands

When it comes to training your Jug, you have to start off slowly with the basic commands. The most popular basic commands for dogs include sit, down, stay, and come.

Sit

This is the most basic, and one of the most important, commands you can teach your Jug.

1.)   Stand in front of your Jug with a few small treats in your pocket.

2.)   Hold one treat in your dominant hand, and wave it in front of your Jug's nose so he gets the scent.

3.)   Give the "Sit" command.

4.)   Move the treat upward and backward over your Jug's head so he is forced to raise his head to follow it.

5.)   In the process, his bottom will lower to the ground.

6.)   As soon as your Jug's bottom hits the ground, praise him and give him the treat.

7.)   Repeat this process several times until your dog gets the hang of it and responds consistently.

Down

After the "Sit" command, "Down" is the next logical command to teach because it is a progression from "Sit."

1.)   Kneel in front of your Jug with a few small treats in your pocket.

2.)   Hold one treat in your dominant hand and give your Jug the "Sit" command.

3.) Reward your Jug for sitting then give him the "Down" command.

4.) Quickly move the treat down to the floor between your Jug's paws.

5.) Your dog will follow the treat and should lie down to retrieve it.

6.) Praise and reward your Jug when he lies down.

7.) Repeat this process several times until your dog gets the hang of it and responds consistently.

Photo: Rocky the Jug

Come

It is very important that your Jug responds to a "come" command because there may come a time when you need to get his attention and call him to your side during a dangerous situation (such as him running around too close to traffic).

1.) Put your Jug on a short leash and stand in front of him.

2.) Give your Jug the "come" command then quickly take a few steps backward away from him.

3.) Clap your hands and act excited, but do not repeat the "come" command.

4.) Keep moving backwards in small steps until your Jug follows and comes to you.

5.) Praise and reward your Jug and repeat the process.

6.) Over time you can use a longer leash or take your Jug off the leash entirely.

7.) You can also start by standing further from your Jug when you give the "come" command.

8.) If your Jug doesn't come to you immediately, you can use the leash to pull him toward you.

Stay

This command is very important because it teaches your Jug discipline – not only does it teach your Jug to stay, but it also forces him to listen/pay attention to you.

1.) Find a friend to help you with this training session.

2.) Have your friend hold your Jug on the leash while you stand in front of the dog.

3.)   Give your Jug the "sit" command and reward him for responding correctly.

4.)   Give your dog the "stay" command while holding your hand out like a "stop" sign.

5.)   Take a few steps backward away from your dog and pause for 1 to 2 seconds.

6.)   Step back toward your Jug then praise and reward your dog.

7.)   Repeat the process several times, then start moving back a little further before you return to your dog.

Photo Credit: John McQuillan

Beyond Basic Training

Once your Jug has a firm grasp on the basics, you can move on to teaching him additional commands. You can also add distractions to the equation to reinforce your dog's mastery of the commands. The end goal is to ensure that your Jug responds to your command each and every time – regardless of distractions and anything else he might rather be doing. This is incredibly important because there may come a time when your dog is in a dangerous situation, and if he doesn't respond to your command, he could get hurt.

After your Jug has started to respond correctly to the basic commands on a regular basis, you can start to incorporate distractions.

If you previously conducted your training sessions indoors, you might consider moving them outside where your dog could be distracted by various sights, smells, and sounds.

One thing you might try is to give your dog the Stay command and then toss a toy nearby that will tempt him to break his Stay. Start by tossing the toy at a good distance from him and wait a few seconds before you release him to play.

Eventually you will be able to toss a toy right next to your dog without him breaking his Stay until you give him permission to do so.

Incorporating Hand Signals

Teaching your Jug to respond to hand signals in addition to verbal commands is very useful – you never know when you will be in a situation where your dog might not be able to hear you.

To start out, choose your dominant hand to give the hand signals and hold a small treat in that hand while you are training your dog – this will encourage your dog to focus on your hand during training, and it will help to cement the connection between the command and the hand signal.

To begin, give your dog the Sit or Down command while holding the treat in your dominant hand and give the appropriate hand signal – for Sit you might try a closed fist, and for Down, you might place your hand flat, parallel to the ground.

When your dog responds correctly, give him the treat. You will need to repeat this process many times in order for your dog to form a connection between both the verbal command and the hand signal with the desired behavior.

Eventually you can start to remove the verbal command from the equation – use the hand gesture every time, but start to use the verbal command only half the time.

Once your dog gets the hang of this, you should start to remove the food reward from the equation. Continue to give your dog the hand signal for each command and occasionally use the verbal command just to remind him.

You should start to phase out the food rewards, however, by offering them only half the time. Progressively lessen the use of the food reward, but continue to praise your dog for performing the behavior correctly so he learns to repeat it.

Teaching Distance Commands

In addition to getting your dog to respond to hand signals, it is also useful to teach him to respond to your commands even when you are not directly next to him.

This may come in handy if your dog is running around outside and gets too close to the street – you should be able to give him a Sit or Down command so he stops before he gets into a dangerous situation.

Teaching your dog distance commands is not difficult, but it does require some time and patience.

To start, give your Jug a brief refresher course of the basic commands while you are standing or kneeling right next to him.

Next, give your dog the Sit and Stay commands then move a few feet away before you give the Come command.

Repeat this process, increasing the distance between you and your dog before giving him the Come command. Be sure to praise and reward your dog for responding appropriately when he does so.

Once your dog gets the hang of coming on command from a distance, you can start to incorporate other commands.

One method of doing so is to teach your dog to sit when you grab his collar. To do so, let your dog wander freely and every once in a while walk up and grab his collar while giving the Sit command.

After a few repetitions, your dog should begin to respond with a Sit when you grab his collar, even if you do not give the command.

Gradually you can increase the distance from which you come to grab his collar and give him the command.

After your dog starts to respond consistently when you come from a distance to grab his collar, you can start giving the Sit command without moving toward him.

It may take your dog a few times to get the hang of it, so be patient. If your dog doesn't Sit right away, calmly walk up to him and repeat the Sit command, but do not grab his collar this time.

Eventually your dog will get the hang of it, and you can start to practice using other commands like Down and Stay from a distance.

Clicker Training

When it comes to training your Jug, you are going to be most successful if you maintain consistency.

Jugs have a tendency to be a little stubborn, so unless you are very clear with your dog about what your expectations are, he may simply decide not to follow your commands.

A simple way to achieve consistency in training your Jug is to use the principles of clicker training. Clicker training involves using a small handheld device that makes a clicking noise when you press it between your fingers.

Clicker training is based on the theory of operant conditioning, which helps your dog to make the connection between the desired behavior and the offering of a reward.

Jugs have a natural desire to please, so if they learn that a certain behavior earns your approval, they will be eager to repeat it – clicker training is a great way to help your dog quickly identify the particular behavior you want him to repeat.

All you have to do is give your Jug a command, and as soon as he performs the behavior, you use the clicker. After you use the clicker, give your dog the reward as you would with any form of positive reinforcement training.

Some of the benefits of clicker training include:

- Very easy to implement – all you need is the clicker.

- Helps your dog form a connection between the command and the desired behavior more quickly.

- You only need to use the clicker until your dog makes the connection, then you can stop.

- May help to keep your dog's attention more effectively if he hears the noise.

Clicker training is just one method of positive reinforcement training that you can consider for training your Jug.

No matter what method you choose, it is important that you maintain consistency and always praise and reward your dog for responding to your commands correctly so he learns to repeat the behavior.

First Tricks

When teaching your Jug their first tricks, in order to give them extra incentive, find a small treat that they would do anything to get, and give the treat as rewards to help solidify a good performance.

Most dogs will be extra attentive during training sessions when they know that they will be rewarded with their favorite treats.

If your Jug is less than six months old when you begin teaching them tricks, keep your training sessions short (no more than 5 or 10 minutes) and make the sessions lots of fun.

As your Jug becomes an adult, you can extend your sessions because they will be able to maintain their focus for longer periods of time.

Photo Credit: Jimtography

Shake a Paw

Who doesn't love a dog who knows how to shake a paw? This is one of the easiest tricks to teach your Jug.

Practice every day until they are 100% reliable with this trick, and then it will be time to add another trick to their repertoire.

Most dogs are naturally either right or left pawed. If you know which paw your dog favors, ask them to shake this paw.

Find a quiet place to practice, without noisy distractions or other pets, and stand or sit in front of your dog. Place them in the sitting position and hold a treat in your left hand.

Say the command "Shake" while putting your right hand behind their left or right paw and pulling the paw gently toward yourself until you are holding their paw in your hand. Immediately praise them and give them the treat.

Most dogs will learn the "Shake" trick very quickly, and in no time at all, once you put out your hand, your Jug will immediately lift their paw and put it into your hand, without your assistance or any verbal cue.

Roll Over

You will find that just like your Jug is naturally either right or left pawed, that they will also naturally want to roll either to the right or the left side.

Take advantage of this by asking your dog to roll to the side they naturally prefer.

Sit with your dog on the floor and put them in a lie down position.

Hold a treat in your hand and place it close to their nose without allowing them to grab it, and while they are in the lying position, move the treat to the right or left side of their head so that they have to roll over to get to it.

You will quickly see which side they want to naturally roll to; once you see this, move the treat to that side. Once they roll over to that side, immediately give them the treat and praise them.

You can say the verbal cue "Over" while you demonstrate the hand signal motion (moving your right hand in a half circular motion) from one side of their head to the other.

Sit Pretty

While this trick is a little more complicated, and most dogs pick up on it very quickly, remember that this trick requires balance, and every dog is different, so always exercise patience.

Find a quiet space with few distractions and sit or stand in front of your dog and ask them to "Sit."

Have a treat nearby (on a countertop or table) and when they sit, use both of your hands to lift up their front paws into the sitting pretty position, while saying the command "Sit Pretty." Help them balance in this position while you praise them and give them the treat.

Once your Jug can do the balancing part of the trick quite easily without your help, sit or stand in front of your dog while asking them to "Sit Pretty" and hold the treat above their head, at the level their nose would be when they sit pretty.

If they attempt to stand on their back legs to get the treat, you may be holding the treat too high, which will encourage them to stand up on their back legs to reach it. Go back to the first step and put them back into the "Sit" position and again lift their paws while their backside remains on the floor.

The hand signal for "Sit Pretty" is a straight arm held over your dog's head with a closed fist.

Place your Jug beside a wall when first teaching this trick so that they can use the wall to help their balance.

A young Jug puppy should be able to easily learn these basic tricks before they are six months old, and when you are patient and make your training sessions short and fun for your dog, they will be eager to learn more.

Dealing with Problem Behaviors

In reading this book, you have heard mention of "small dog syndrome" several times in connection with the Jug breed.

Both Pugs and Jack Russell Terriers have a tendency to become a little stubborn, especially in cases where training is not consistent, so you need to be on the lookout for this condition with your dog.

You should also keep an eye out for the development of certain problem behaviors such as excessive digging, barking, or chewing.

In this section, you will learn how to effectively deal with these problem behaviors.

Most behaviors that dog owners identify as problems are actually behaviors that are completely natural for dogs. It is natural for your dog to dig, to bark, and to chew on things – it only becomes a problem when that behavior is exhibited in a destructive way.

The best way to deal with these problems, then, is not to try to eradicate them entirely but to redirect them to a more appropriate outlet.

Digging

Jack Russell Terriers have a natural instinct for digging because they were bred to root foxes out of their holes. If you do not provide your Jug with enough exercise, or if you do not train him properly, he may develop a problem with digging in your yard at home.

Rather than discouraging your dog from digging entirely, the better option is to redirect his digging behavior toward a more appropriate outlet.

If you don't want your Jug to dig up your flower beds, try creating a small section of the yard where it is okay for him to dig.

Encourage your dog to dig in this area by burying toys or treats in the ground so he learns that digging in this area is more fun than digging up your flowers.

If you catch your Jug digging somewhere he shouldn't be, tell him No in a firm voice and lead him to the spot where he is allowed to dig. When he starts playing in that area, praise and reward him for good behavior.

Barking

For the most part, neither Pugs nor Jack Russell Terriers are yappy breeds, but if your dog learns that barking gets him the attention he wants, he may be more likely to do it.

For example, if your Jug has a tendency to bark when the doorbell rings, and then whoever comes through the door rewards him by petting him, he will only learn to repeat that behavior.

Due to their Jack Russell Terrier blood, Jugs may also develop a tendency to bark at squirrels, rabbits, and other animals that come into the yard.

The first step to teaching your Jug not to bark is to teach him to bark on command – then you can teach him a command to stop barking.

To do so, you will need the help of a friend or family member. Have that person stand outside your door, ready to ring the doorbell.

Give your Jug a "Speak" command and have your friend immediately ring the doorbell to get your dog to bark.

When he does, reward him with praise and a treat. After a few barks, give your dog the "Hush" or "Quiet" command and reward him when he stops barking.

If your dog doesn't immediately stop barking, try waving the treat in front of his nose to catch his attention.

Chewing

Jugs tend to become bored easily, so if you do not give your dog enough exercise or attention, he may develop a problem with destructive chewing.

In some cases, chewing behavior develops as a symptom of separation anxiety – your dog may become nervous about being left alone and resort to chewing as a way to work out his anxiety.

In most cases, however, chewing is simply a behavior that dogs develop because they are bored.

The key to dealing with chewing behavior is to redirect it to a more appropriate outlet. Make sure your dog has plenty of chew toys to choose from – try using a variety of toys, including Kong toys that you can fill with treats like peanut butter.

When you catch your Jug chewing on something he shouldn't be, take the item away while saying No in a firm voice.

Immediately give your dog one of his toys, and praise him when he begins to chew on it instead. Eventually your dog will learn what he is and is not allowed to chew on.

Photo Credit: John McQuillan

Socialization

Generally speaking, the majority of an adult dog's habits and behavioral traits will be formed between the ages of birth and one year of age.

This is why it will be very important to introduce your Jug puppy to a wide variety of animals, locations, sights, sounds, and smells during this formative period in their young life.

Your Jug puppy will learn how to behave in all these various circumstances by following your lead, feeling your energy, and watching how you react in every situation. For instance, never accidentally reward your Jug puppy for displaying fear or growling at another dog or animal by picking them up.

Picking up a Jug puppy or dog at this time, when they are displaying unbalanced energy, actually turns out to be a reward for them, and you will be teaching them to continue with this type of behavior. As well, picking up a puppy literally places them in a "top dog" position, where they are higher and more dominant than the dog or animal they just growled at.

The correct action to take in such a situation is to gently correct your puppy with a firm yet calm energy by distracting them with a "No," so that they learn to let you deal with the situation on their behalf.

If you allow a fearful or nervous puppy to deal with situations that unnerve them all by themselves, they may learn to react with fear or aggression, and you will have created a problem that could escalate into something quite serious as they grow older.

The same is true of situations where a young puppy may feel the need to protect themselves from a bigger or older dog that may come charging in for a sniff.

It is the guardian's responsibility to protect the puppy, so that they do not think they must react with fear or aggression in order to protect themselves.

Once your Jug puppy has received all their vaccinations, you can take them out to public dog parks and various locations where many dogs are found.

Before allowing them to interact with other dogs or puppies, take them for a disciplined walk on leash, so that they will be a little tired and less likely to immediately engage with all other dogs.

Keep your puppy on leash and close beside you, because most puppies are usually a bundle of out-of-control energy, and you need to protect them while teaching them how far they can go before getting themselves into trouble with adult dogs who may not appreciate excited puppy playfulness.

If your puppy shows any signs of aggression or domination toward another puppy or dog, you must immediately step in and calmly discipline them; by doing nothing, you will be allowing them to get into situations that could become serious behavioral issues.

Take your puppy everywhere with you and introduce them to many different people of all ages, sizes, and ethnicities.

Most people will come to you and want to interact with your puppy. If they ask if they can hold your puppy, let them; if they are gentle and don't drop the puppy, this is a good way to socialize your Jug and show them that humans are friendly.

Do not let others (especially children) play roughly with your puppy or squeal at them in high-pitched voices, because this can be very frightening for a young puppy.

Be careful when introducing your puppy to young children who don't know how to act around a puppy and who may accidentally hurt your puppy. You don't want them to become fearful of children, as this could lead to aggression later on in life.

Explain to children that your Jug puppy is very young and that they must be calm and gentle when playing or interacting.

As important as socialization is, it is also important that the dog be left alone for short periods when young so that they can cope with some periods of isolation. If an owner goes out and they have never experienced this, they can destroy things and make a mess because they panic. They are thinking that they are vulnerable and can be attacked by something or someone coming in to the house.

Dogs that have been socialized are able to easily diffuse a potentially troublesome situation and hence they will rarely get into fights. Dogs that are poorly socialized often misinterpret or do not understand the subtle signals of other dogs, getting into trouble as a result.

Photo Credit: Sadie by Barbra Baker

Chapter 6 - Breeding Your Jug

Breeding your dog can be an exciting yet challenging experience, and it is certainly not one that you should enter into lightly.

The decision to breed your Jugs is one that you should take slowly and for the right reasons – do not breed your jugs simply because you are curious to see what it will be like.

In this chapter, you will learn the basics about breeding your Jugs, including tips for encouraging mating, the signs of pregnancy, and how to care for then wean the puppies when they are born.

Photo Credit: Sergei by Mercedes Clark-Smith

Basic Breeding Information

The first thing you need to do before you breed your Jugs is to establish your reason for doing so.

It is a common misconception that breeding dogs is a great way to make some extra money. In reality, however, you are unlikely to make a profit on your puppies after you factor in the costs of care for the pregnant female and the cost to raise and care for the puppies until they are ready to sell.

If, on the other hand, you want to breed your Jugs for love of and concern about the preservation of the breed, that is a better reason for breeding.

Before you start breeding your Jugs, there is some basic information you should know about them in regard to breeding. Different dog breeds can be bred at different ages and birth litters of different sizes.

Age of First Heat: around 5 to 6 months
Sexual Maturity (male): 6 to 12 months
Sexual Maturity (female): 6 to 9 months
Breeding Age (male): 9 to 10 months
Breeding Age (female): about 1 year
Physical Maturity: about 12 months
Heat (Estrus) Cycle: 14 to 21 days
Frequency: twice a year, every 6 months
Ovulation: 7 to 10 days into the cycle
Gestation Period: about 63 days (9 weeks)
Pregnancy Detection: after 3 weeks
Litter Size: 3 to 8

Before you can breed your Jugs, you have to wait for both the male and female to reach sexual maturity. For females, this typically happens between 6 and 9 months of age – that is when the dog will experience her first estrus, or "heat," cycle. This does not, however, mean that she is ready to breed.

Most breeders recommend waiting until a female dog is about 1 year old before breeding her.

Males, on the other hand, become sexually mature anywhere between 6 and 12 months and can be bred as early as 9 or 10 months of age, as long as they have reached maturity.

For females, the estrus cycle is simply the period of time during which the body is receptive to and capable of breeding.

This cycle typically occurs twice a year, about every 6 months, and lasts for 2 to 3 weeks. By the 7 to 10th day of the cycle, the female will ovulate – this is when conception (pregnancy) can actually occur.

If you are going to breed your Jugs, you need to learn to recognize the signs of estrus and learn to judge when your female is starting to ovulate.

Signs of Estrus:

- Swelling of the external vulva
- Reddish vaginal discharge
- Increased frequency of urination
- Urine-marking behavior

When your female's vaginal discharge becomes pink and watery around the 7th day of her cycle, it is generally a sign that she is or will soon be ovulating – this is when you want to introduce her to the male.

Ideally, breeding should occur in the male dog's home environment, where he will be the most comfortable. Simply bring your female dog to the male, and they will do the rest of the work themselves.

Note: It is very important that you supervise all breeding activities, because you never know how the two dogs are going to react to one another.

If the female refuses to breed during the first meeting, remove her and try again the next day and the day after that until a successful breeding is accomplished.

Raising the Babies

If a breeding results in conception (pregnancy), the female will go through a gestation period lasting about 63 days (9 weeks). During this time, it is important that you keep a close eye on the female.

You may not be able to palpate the pups in her womb until about 3 weeks after conception, so it is very important that you record the timing of the breeding so you can keep track of the progress.

While your female Jug is in the early stages of pregnancy, you do not need to change anything in regard to her feeding or care.

As the pups develop insider her, however, her energy needs will increase along with her weight. During the 5th week of pregnancy, start to slowly increase her food rations in proportion to her weight gain.

Ideally, you should be feeding several small meals throughout the day at this point as well rather than one or two large meals.

By the end of the pregnancy, your female should only be eating about 40% to 50% more than she was prior to the pregnancy.

As your female approaches the end of her pregnancy, there are a few things you need to do. First, set up a whelping box where she can actually have the puppies.

This box should be large enough for the dog as well as a litter of puppies, and it should be placed in a dark, quiet area where your Jug will feel safe.

Line the box with newspaper and/or towels that you do not mind getting dirty and give the dog some time to get used to it. Ideally, you should set up the box within the last week of pregnancy.

A few days before your Jug gives birth, you may notice the signs of early labor. These signs may include:

- Reduction in appetite/stops eating
- Spends more time in the whelping box
- Body temperature drops (within 24 hours of birth)
- Dilation of the cervix
- Restlessness and panting

For the most part, your female Jug will be able to birth the puppies on her own without any help from you. You should, however, be present for the occasion just in case something should happen.

It would be wise for you to have the number for an emergency vet on hand just in case.

The puppies themselves will be born one at a time, and your Jug will likely pause to clean each puppy after it is born before birthing the next one.

Let your Jug handle this on her own, but keep track of the number of puppies that are born, as well as the number of placenta delivered so you can be sure that all of the afterbirth is delivered.

After all of the puppies have been born and cleaned, the female Jug will allow them to nurse. The first milk a female dog produces is called the colostrum, and it is full of vital nutrients and antibodies that are essential for a newborn puppy to help them fight off infections while their immune systems are still developing.

During the first few weeks of life, the puppies will nurse several times a day, and the mother will lick them to stimulate urination and defecation because newborn puppies are incapable of performing these actions on their own.

After 3 to 4 weeks of nursing, your female Jug may begin to wean the puppies on her own – that is, to transition them from nursing to eating solid food. Two weeks or so after the puppies are born it would be wise to start offering small amounts of puppy food so the puppies can sample it on their own.

To make it easier for the puppies to digest, try wetting it with water or puppy formula. By four weeks of age, the puppies should be almost completely transitioned onto the puppy food, at which point you can separate them from the mother and continue to raise them.

Note: Though Jug puppies are unlikely to reach sexual maturity until 6 months of age or later, it is always wise to separate the sexes after 2 to 3 months. This will help to prevent unwanted breeding.

Chapter 7 - Keeping Your Jug Healthy

Your dog is more than just a pet – he is a member of the family and, quite possibly, your best friend. This being the case, you want to take care of him as much as possible.

Unfortunately, you can't completely prevent your Jug from ever getting sick, but you can learn as much as you can about potential health problems to ensure that your Jug gets the treatment he needs when he needs it.

Photo Credit: Sadie by Barbra Baker

The key to keeping your Jug happy and healthy is to learn everything you can about the potential conditions that could affect him.

The sooner you start treatment for a disease or condition, the greater your Jug's chances of recovery are.

In this section, you will read about some of the most common conditions affecting the Jug breed, as well as their symptoms and treatment options.

Common diseases affecting the Jug breed include:

Allergies
Breathing Problems
Cardiomyopathy
Hip Dysplasia
Legg-Calve Perthes
Lens Luxation
Nerve Degeneration
Patellar Luxation
Progressive Retinal Atrophy
Pug Dog Encephalitis
Von Willebrand Disease
Weeping Eyes

Allergies

The Pug breed is particularly susceptible to developing a number of allergies, so your Jug may be prone to them as well.

Pugs may exhibit all types of allergies, such as skin allergies, food allergies, or even seasonal allergies. Internal allergies, such as those caused by food, typically cause symptoms like vomiting and diarrhea, while external allergies often cause skin problems like itching, redness, and hot spots.

Cause: food sensitivities, pollen, parasites, etc.
Symptoms: itchy skin, redness, hot spots, vomiting, diarrhea
Treatment: topical treatments for external allergies, modified diet for internal allergies

Breathing Problems

Short-faced (brachycephalic) breeds like the Pug are particularly prone to breathing problems, including elongated soft palate (ESP) and stenotic nares.

Depending on the breeding of your Jug, he may have the kind of short, squashed face that encourages these problems.

Elongated soft palate (ESP) is a condition in which the palate is elongated and causes an obstruction in the dog's airway. This may result in gasping for air, honking sounds, and snoring – the condition can generally be corrected through surgery.

Stenotic nares are a birth defect characterized by overly soft nasal tissue. When the dog breathes, the nostrils collapse and interfere with the intake of air. As a result, the dog must breathe through its mouth. This condition can also be corrected through surgery.

Cause: elongated soft palate obstructs airway or collapsed nostrils interfering with inhalation
Symptoms: gasping for air, honking sounds, breathing through the mouth, snoring
Treatment: surgery is generally required

Cardiomyopathy

This is one of the most common heart conditions in dogs.

This disease causes the heart muscle of the dog to become inflamed, which impairs its function. There are two different types of cardiomyopathy – dilated cardiomyopathy and hypertrophic cardiomyopathy.

In cases of dilated cardiomyopathy (DCM), the chambers of the heart increase in size (dilate), which stretches the muscles thin – this is one of the leading causes of heart failure in dogs.

Hypertrophic cardiomyopathy involves thickening of the heart chamber walls, which leads to decreased pumping efficiency.

The causes of cardiomyopathy are unknown, though some breeds have a higher risk than others depending on various factors like low blood potassium levels, toxic injury to the heart, and low blood supply to the heart.

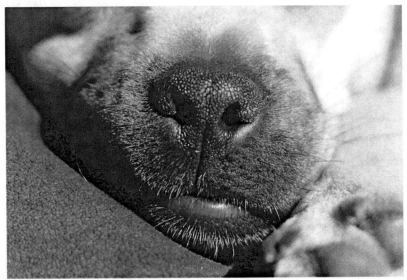

Photo Credit: Grandmaster Flash by Emma Fisher

Symptoms of this condition include shortness of breath, coughing, exercise intolerance, lethargy, and loss of appetite.

Treatment typically involves controlling the symptoms with medications because no cure for the disease is available.

Cause: unknown, various factors may increase a dog's risk

Symptoms: shortness of breath, coughing, exercise intolerance, lethargy, and loss of appetite
Treatment: medication to control symptoms, no cure

Hip Dysplasia

This is a disease that affects the hip joints of many dog breeds, though small breeds are typically less affected than larger breeds.

Hip dysplasia occurs when the head of the femur pops out of or doesn't rest properly within the hip joint. This results in pain and discomfort in movement, as well as progressive osteoarthritis. If the condition isn't treated, it can result in lameness in the leg.

This condition can be treated either medically or surgically, depending on the severity of the case.

Because hip dysplasia is a hereditary condition, its development cannot be prevented, but the use of anti-inflammatory medications can help decrease its progression.

Surgical corrections for the condition are also possible to repair the problem with the bone and joint.

Cause: congenital (inherited), femur head pops out of the hip joint
Symptoms: pain and discomfort in movement, progressive osteoarthritis, lameness
Treatment: anti-inflammatory medications to manage pain, surgical corrections are often necessary

Legg-Calve Perthes

This is a condition that affects the hip joints of certain breeds, including the Jack Russell Terrier and other toy breeds.

This condition results in the obstruction of blood supply to the femur bone, which then causes the head of the femur itself to deteriorate over time. This disease typically manifests early, between 4 and 6 months of age, and it may present in the form of a limp or atrophied leg muscle.

The cause of this disease is unknown, and it is possible for it to come on without warning. If the condition isn't treated, it can progress to severe pain, restricted movement, wasting of the thigh muscle, and eventual lameness in the affected leg.

When the case is minor, the symptoms can be managed with pain medication and exercise of the femur.

As the disease progresses, however, surgery may be the only option. With surgery and physical therapy, a 3 to 6 month recovery period can be expected.

Cause: unknown cause, deterioration of the head of the femur bone
Symptoms: pain, restricted movement, wasting of thigh muscle, lameness in affected leg
Treatment: pain medication and physical therapy, surgical correction may be needed

Lens Luxation

This is a common eye problem that affects the Jack Russell Terrier breed. Depending on your Jug's breeding, he could also be at risk for developing this condition.

Lens luxation is a hereditary condition characterized by the dislocation of the lens of the eye. Symptoms may include discharge or reddening of the eye, along with an inability or difficulty in opening the eye.

In severe cases, lens luxation can lead to permanent blindness –
that is why it is essential that you seek treatment for this
condition as early as possible.

Some cases can be treated with medication or surgery. It simply
depends on the severity of the case. In the event that blindness
occurs, however, dogs are generally able to adapt well to the loss
of sight.

Cause: congenital (inherited), lens of the eye becomes dislocated
Symptoms: discharge, redness, difficulty opening the eye, loss of
vision
Treatment: medication may help, but surgery is often needed to
repair the problem

Nerve Degeneration

Also referred to as degenerative myelopathy, nerve degeneration
is a condition that is fairly common in older pugs – as your Jug
ages, you should keep an eye out for signs of this condition.

Nerve degeneration is a progressive disease that leads to
weakness and paralysis in the hindquarters. Over time, the parts
of the spinal cord that are responsible for nerve impulses break
down, which leads to increased difficulty in muscle control and
coordination.

Symptoms of this condition include awkward movement,
dragging the feet, and eventual inability to walk.

This disease typically affects dogs over the age of 5, and it takes
several months to a year to fully set in. Unfortunately, there is no
cure for this condition, but the symptoms can be managed
through physical therapy.

Cause: degeneration of spinal cord, weakened nerve impulses
Symptoms: awkward movement, dragging the feet, and eventual inability to walk
Treatment: no cure, though physical therapy may help with management of symptoms

Patellar Luxation

This condition affects the patella, or kneecap, of the dog, and it is a fairly common condition in many breeds.

Patellar luxation is characterized by the dislocation of the kneecap – it doesn't return to its normal position in the groove of the femur bone as it should.

Symptoms of this condition may vary depending on the severity of the case, but they usually include pain and difficulty moving. In more severe cases, this condition can lead to lameness.

There are two causes for this condition – it can either be inherited or caused by injury to the leg. When the condition is hereditary, it typically manifests by 4 months of age.

In mild cases, medical management of symptoms may be possible, but surgery is generally required to correct the problem and to prevent lameness.

Cause: congenital (inherited) or injury to the leg, involves dislocation of the knee cap
Symptoms: pain, difficulty moving, lameness
Treatment: medication for pain management, surgical correction is often needed

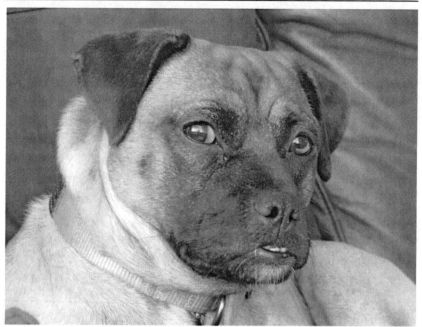

Photo: Jug - Peanut

Progressive Retinal Atrophy

This condition is a disease affecting the eye, and it is also simply referred to as PRA. Progressive retinal atrophy is an inherited eye disorder that commonly affects the Pug breed. Though the condition is not painful, it can lead to eventual blindness.

During the initial stages of PRA, affected dogs may exhibit dilated pupils and increased eye shine. As it progresses, many dogs develop night blindness.

Once PRA progresses to the point where night blindness occurs, it is really only a matter of time before the dog's day vision is affected as well.

Signs of vision loss include difficulty dealing with changes in the home (such as rearranging furniture) and your dog failing to wander as far as he used to on walks and in the yard. There is no treatment for PRA, but most dogs that develop vision loss are able to adapt well.

Cause: congenital (inherited)
Symptoms: dilated pupils, increased eye shine, night blindness, loss of vision
Treatment: no treatment available

Pug Dog Encephalitis

Also referred to as PDA, Pug Dog Encephalitis is a condition that commonly affects the Pug breed. Because the Jug is a hybrid of the Pug and Jack Russell Terrier, there is a possibility that this breed could also be affected.

PDE is characterized by inflammation of the brain, which typically affects young to middle-aged dogs.

Symptoms of this condition include seizures, lethargy, listlessness, and loss of muscle coordination.

The progression of this disease varies from one case to another – in one case it may move slowly, while in another it may progress rapidly. In slow-moving cases, the dog may return to normal between seizures, but in rapid cases, the dog may become increasingly disoriented between seizures.

Unfortunately there is no cure for this disease, but medication can be used to control the symptoms and corticosteroids may be administered to reduce inflammation in the brain.

Cause: inflammation of the brain
Symptoms: seizures, lethargy, listlessness, loss of muscle control

Treatment: no cure available, steroids or other medications may be used to control seizures and reduce inflammation

Von Willebrand Disease

This is a blood disease caused by a deficiency of von Willebrand Factor, or vWF. Von Willebrand Factor is a type of adhesive glycoprotein that is required for normal platelet binding and clotting.

An affected dog may have trouble forming blood clots and, as a result, may bleed profusely from even the slightest injury.

Jack Russell Terriers are one of the breeds affected by this disease, and since it is hereditary, there is a possibility that your Jug could be affected as well.

Some of the symptoms include excessive bleeding for minor injuries, nosebleeds, bleeding gums, and blood in the feces.

Unfortunately there is no cure for this disease, but there are several management options, including blood transfusions to treat blood loss.

Cause: congenital (inherited), deficiency of von Willebrand Factor (vWF)
Symptoms: excessive bleeding from minor injury, nosebleeds, bleeding gums, blood in feces, not clotting
Treatment: transfusion to treat blood loss, no cure available for the disease itself

Weeping Eyes

Also referred to as Epiphora, or excessive tearing, weeping eyes is a condition that is very common in the Pug breed.

Depending on your Jug's breeding, he may be at risk for this condition as well. It is important to realize that weeping eyes is not a condition in and of itself but a symptom of another problem, such as inflammation, allergies, corneal ulcers, glaucoma, or distichiasis (ingrown eyelashes).

Dogs with this problem typically exhibit excessive tearing and staining at the corner of the eyes. In most cases, the discharge from the eye is clear and watery – if it is thick or colored, it could be an indication of a serious infection.

The treatment for this condition depends on the underlying cause, but it is generally fairly easy to clean up.

Cause: inflammation, allergies, corneal ulcer, glaucoma, distichiasis
Symptoms: excessive tearing, staining at the corner of the eye, irritation of the eye
Treatment: treatment for underlying cause

Preventing Illness

Understanding the common conditions that affect the Jug breed is the key to preventing your dog from getting them.

No matter how informed you are, however, your dog could still come into contact with disease – that is where vaccines come in. Vaccines are the best way to protect your dog in the event that he is exposed to a disease.

In addition to having your Jug vaccinated, you should also schedule regular check-ups with your veterinarian.

Your Jug should receive a full examination at least once but ideally twice a year. During this exam, your vet should check your Jug's weight, eyes, ears, teeth, and run any blood tests he thinks are necessary. You will also receive recommendations for vaccinations during this exam.

Refer to the chart below to see what vaccinations your Jug needs:

Recommended Vaccination Schedule			
Vaccine	Doses	Age	Booster
Rabies	1	12 weeks	annual
Distemper	3	6-16 weeks	3 years
Parvovirus	3	6-16 weeks	3 years
Adenovirus	3	6-16 weeks	3 years
Parainfluenza	3	6 weeks, 12-14 weeks	3 years
Bordatella	1		annual
Lyme Disease	2	9, 13-14 weeks	annual
Leptospirosis	2	12 and 16 weeks	annual
Canine Influenza	2	6-8, 8-12 weeks	annual

Working With Your Veterinarian

If you do not already have a veterinarian with whom you work, finding a qualified doctor is the first step in ensuring your dog's long-term good health. Ask your breeder for a recommendation, or if you have worked with a kennel outside of your immediate area, try to connect with other Jug owners in your locale.

Photo Credit: Frank by Tim Webb

Make an appointment to go into the clinic to see the facility and meet the vet. Be clear that you are there to discuss becoming a client and will happily pay the fee for a visit. Prepare your questions in advance so you don't waste anyone's time — including your own. Some questions you will want answered include:

- How long has your clinic been open?
- What hours do you operate?
- What medical services do you offer?
- What grooming services do you offer?
- Do you have an estimated schedule of fees?
- How many vets are on staff?
- Do you provide emergency services after hours?
- Is there an emergency vet clinic you recommend?
- Are there any specialists in your practice?

- Where do you refer dogs in need of a specialist?
- Do you currently treat any Jugs?

Pay attention to how you are greeted when you arrive at the clinic. Does the staff seem friendly and approachable? Are they well organized? Is there a bulletin board in the waiting room with notes and photos from patients? If so, that's always a good sign of a satisfied clientele. Does the facility seem modern and up to date? Is it clean, airy, and light? Are the doctor's credentials prominently displayed?

First Visit to the Vet

If you are satisfied with the answers you receive and what you see on your tour of the clinic, schedule a second visit to come in with your puppy. Bring all medical records with you, since you will likely be discussing completing the dog's required vaccinations and arranging to have him spayed or neutered.

The routine examination will include a reading of the dog's temperature and a check of heart and lung function with a stethoscope. The puppy will be weighed and measured for its permanent record. If you have any questions about Jug health moving forward, try to have them prepared in advance so you don't forget anything.

Vaccinations

A usual course of vaccinations begins when a puppy is 6-7 weeks of age. The first shot is a combination inoculation for distemper, hepatitis, parvovirus, parainfluenza, and coronavirus. Boosters are administered at 9, 12, and 16 weeks. Depending on the area, a vaccine for Lyme Disease may be started at 16 weeks, with a booster required at 18 weeks.

The rabies vaccination is administered at 12-16 weeks of age and annually for life thereafter.

DAPP Vaccinations

All puppies are vaccinated by a licensed veterinarian in order to provide them with protection against the four most common and serious diseases, which include Distemper, Adenovirus, Parainfluenza, and Parvovirus. This set of four primary vaccinations is referred to as "DAPP."

Approximately one week after your Jug puppy has completed all three sets of DAPP vaccinations, they will be fully protected from these four specific diseases. Then, most veterinarians will recommend a once-a-year vaccination for the next year or two.

Distemper

Canine distemper is a contagious and serious viral illness for which there is currently no known cure.

This deadly virus, which is spread either through the air or by direct or indirect contact with a dog that is already infected, or other distemper-carrying wildlife, including ferrets, raccoons, foxes, skunks, and wolves, is a relative of the measles virus that affects humans.

Canine distemper is sometimes also called "hard pad disease," because some strains of the distemper virus actually cause thickening of the pads on a dog's feet, which can also affect the end of a dog's nose.

In dogs or animals with weak immune systems, death may result two to five weeks after the initial infection.

Early symptoms of distemper include fever, loss of appetite, and mild eye inflammation that may only last a day or two.

Symptoms become more serious and noticeable as the disease progresses.

A puppy or dog that survives the distemper virus will usually continue to experience symptoms or signs of the disease throughout their remaining lifespan, including "hard pad disease" as well as "enamel hypoplasia," which is damage to the enamel of the puppy's teeth that are not yet formed or that have not yet pushed through the gums.

Enamel hypoplasia is caused by the distemper virus killing the cells that manufacture tooth enamel.

Adenovirus

This virus causes infectious canine hepatitis, which can range in severity from very mild to very serious, or even cause death.

Symptoms can include coughing, loss of appetite, increased thirst and urination, tiredness, runny eyes and nose, vomiting, bruising or bleeding under the skin, swelling of the head, neck and trunk, fluid accumulation in the abdomen area, jaundice (yellow tinge to the skin), a bluish clouding of the cornea of the eye (called "hepatitis blue eye"), and seizures.

There is no specific treatment for infectious canine hepatitis, and treatment is focused on managing symptoms while the virus runs its course.

Hospitalization and intravenous fluid therapy may be required in severe cases.

Parainfluenza Virus

The canine parainfluenza virus originally affected only horses but has now adapted to become contagious to dogs. Also referred to as "canine influenza virus," "greyhound disease," or "race flu," it is easily spread from dog to dog through the air or by coming into contact with respiratory secretions from an infected animal.

While the more frequent occurrences of this respiratory infection are seen in areas with high dog populations, such as race tracks, boarding kennels, and pet stores, this virus is highly contagious to any dog or puppy, regardless of age.

Symptoms can include a dry, hacking cough, difficulty breathing, wheezing, runny nose and eyes, sneezing, fever, loss of appetite, tiredness, depression, and possible pneumonia.

In cases where only a cough exists, tests will be required to determine whether the cause of the cough is the parainfluenza virus or the less serious "kennel cough."

While many dogs can naturally recover from this virus, they will remain contagious. For this reason, to prevent the spread to other animals, aggressive treatment of the virus with antibiotics and antiviral drugs will be the prescribed course of action.

In more severe cases, a cough suppressant may be used, as well as intravenous fluids to prevent secondary bacterial infection.

Parvovirus

Canine parvovirus is a highly contagious viral illness affecting puppies and dogs that also affects other canine species, including foxes, coyotes, and wolves.

There are two forms of this virus — (1) the more common intestinal form and (2) the less common cardiac form, which can cause death in young puppies.

Symptoms of the intestinal form of parvovirus include vomiting, bloody diarrhea, weight loss, and lack of appetite, while the less common cardiac form attacks the heart muscle.

Photo Credit: Jimtography

Early vaccination in young puppies has radically reduced the incidence of canine parvovirus infection, which is easily transmitted either by direct contact with an infected dog, or indirectly, by sniffing an infected dog's feces.

The virus can also be brought into a dog's environment on the bottom of human shoes that may have stepped on infected feces, and there is evidence that this hardy virus can live in ground soil for up to a year.

Recovery from parvovirus requires both aggressive and early treatment. With proper treatment, death rates are relatively low (between 5 and 20%), although chances of survival for puppies are much lower than older dogs, and in all instances, there is no guarantee of survival.

Treatment of parvovirus requires hospitalization, where intravenous fluids and nutrients are administered to help combat dehydration.

As well, antibiotics will be given to counteract secondary bacterial infections, and as necessary, medications to control nausea and vomiting may be given.

Without prompt and proper treatment, dogs that have severe parvovirus infections can die within 48 to 72 hours.

Rabies Vaccinations

Rabies is a viral disease transmitted through the saliva of an infected animal, usually through a bite. The virus travels to the brain along the nerves, and once symptoms develop, death is almost certainly inevitable, usually following a prolonged period of suffering.

Leishmaniasis

Leishmaniasis is caused by a parasite and is transmitted by a bite from a sand fly. There is no definitive answer for effectively combating leishmaniasis, especially since one vaccine will not prevent the known multiple species.

Note: Leishmaniasis is a "zoonotic" infection, which means that this is a contagious disease, and that organisms residing in the Leishmaniasis lesions can be spread between animals and humans and, ultimately, transmitted to humans.

Lyme Disease

This is one of the most common tick-borne diseases in the world, which is transmitted by Borrelia bacteria found in the deer or sheep tick. Lyme disease, also called "borreliosis," can affect both humans and dogs, and can be fatal.

There is a vaccine for Lyme disease, and dogs living in areas that have easy access to these ticks should be vaccinated yearly.

Evaluating for Worms

Before your puppy's first visit with the vet, you will be asked to collect a fresh stool sample, which will be tested for worms. If any parasites are found, the puppy will be given an initial deworming agent, followed by a second course in 10 days, to make sure any remaining eggs have been killed.

It is unlikely that a puppy purchased from a breeder will have worms, but a rescue dog might. Typically, the only external signs of roundworms are small white granules around the anus. Other worms can only be detected with microscopic examination. Tapeworms in particular can be life threatening and require veterinary treatment.

De-worming kills internal parasites that your dog or puppy has, and no matter where you live, how sanitary your conditions, or how much of a neat freak you are, your dog will have internal parasites, because it is not a matter of cleanliness.

It is recommended by the Centers for Disease Control and Prevention (CDC) that puppies be de-wormed every 2 weeks until they are 3 months old, and then every month after that in order to control worms.

Many veterinarians recommend worming dogs for tapeworm and roundworms every 6-12 months.

Spaying and Neutering

Spaying or neutering your Jug puppy is typically a requirement of the adoption agreement. These procedures, however, beyond eliminating unwanted pregnancies, also carry significant health benefits for your pet.

Neutered males face a reduced risk of prostatic disease or perianal tumors. The surgery also reduces many aggressive behaviors and lessens the dog's territorial instinct. He will be less likely to mark territory or to behave inappropriately against the legs of your visitors.

Spayed females no longer face the prospect of uterine or ovarian cancer and have a diminished risk for breast cancer. You will not have to deal with your pet coming into season, nor will she experience hormone-related mood swings.

Neutering and spaying surgeries are typically performed around six months of age. The procedures don't make the dogs any more prone to gain weight.

"Normal" Health Issues

Although Jug are, on a whole, happy and healthy, there are some issues that can arise that should be treated by or evaluated by a veterinarian to be on the safe side. Anytime that your dog seems inattentive or lethargic and stops eating or drinking water, seek medical attention for your pet immediately.

Note: Any gastrointestinal upset in dogs can be linked to ingestion of toxic household or garden plants.

Photo Credit: Jugs - Peanut & Cuthbert

Diarrhea

Jug puppies have sensitive digestive systems that can be upset by any disruption in their diet, from eating human food to getting into the garbage. This will result in diarrhea (watery and frequent bowel movements).

Typically an instance of diarrhea caused by one of these factors will resolve on its own within 24 hours after the offending food has passed out of the animal's system.

During episodes of diarrhea, give your puppy only small amounts of dry food and do not include any treats. It is imperative the puppy have access to fresh, clean water. If the condition has not improved in 24 hours, take the dog to the vet.

Even adult dogs will sometimes have occasional gastrointestinal upset that manifests as diarrhea. Typically this is not a serious health concern, so long as the episode resolves in a day. Any chronic or prolonged condition, however, is another matter.

For chronic, episodic diarrhea, the cause is typically dietary and often linked to an over-abundance of rich, fatty food. Try switching to a food that is lower in fat, with less protein. Smaller portions and more frequent feedings are also indicated.

If you suspect that the cause of the upset is an allergy, consider having your dog tested so you can find the right food. Many small dogs are allergic to chicken and turkey, for instance.

There is always the possibility that the diarrhea is being caused by some pathogen, either a bacteria or a virus. If vomiting and a fever are also present, your pet is likely suffering from an infection and requires veterinary attention.

Finally, your dog may need to be wormed. Both tapeworm and roundworm can cause instances of diarrhea.

Vomiting

Vomiting, like diarrhea, may also be a sign of a change in diet or an indication that the puppy has gotten into something that didn't agree with him. So long as the dog is actually throwing up and getting the substance out of his system, the issue should resolve in about 24 hours.

However, if the dog is attempting to vomit and cannot expel anything, if there's any trace of blood in the material that is expelled, or if your pet cannot even keep water down, call the vet immediately.

Dehydration is a dangerous and potentially fatal condition and may require the administration of intravenous fluids.

Always examine the area where the dog has been and try to identify anything with signs of chewing, or any item that is missing and might have been swallowed. This may help both you and the vet to get a handle on the cause of the dog's illness.

Other potential causes of vomiting include the presence of hookworm or roundworm, pancreatitis (inflammation of the pancreas), diabetes, thyroid disease, kidney disease, liver disease, or some sort of physical obstruction that has caused a blockage. In this latter instance, surgery may be necessary.

In cases of both diarrhea and/or vomiting, you can add white rice to your dog's regular food after 48 hours to improve the consistency of the stools and to settle ongoing stomach upset. Generally you can resume your pet's regular diet after 72 hours.

Bloat

Bloat occurs when a puppy eats too quickly and, in the process, swallows large amounts of air that fill up the stomach and cause it to become swollen. If the stomach turns with gastric torsion, the flow of blood in the abdomen will be cut off, causing shock and death.

The symptoms of bloat include distension of the abdomen, dry vomiting, and coughing after eating.

If you suspect your puppy is suffering from bloat, seek the aid of a qualified veterinary professional immediately.

Bloat can be avoided by feeding the dog several small meals each day in a quiet, distraction-free environment and by not allowing the animal to exercise for at least an hour after eating.

Allergies

Dogs of any age can suffer from allergies. These may be either environmental or substance-based to items like cleaning solutions, laundry soap, or fabric softeners. Puppies come into contact with this type of chemical most often in their bedding, but they can also rub against things in your home and be exposed to the irritant.

Typical canine responses to allergic reactions include scratching, licking, and chewing, but this behavior will differ from a response to fleas. With fleas the dog will scratch or chew intermittently, but with allergies, they will worry at the spot constantly, often causing patches of hair loss and the eruption of skin rashes.

Begin by washing your dog's bedding in perfume-free detergent and do not use dryer sheets. If anything new has come into the house against which the dog might be rubbing, temporarily remove the item. Also, if you have switched to a new brand or flavor of food, go back to what the puppy was eating previously.

In instances where you cannot discover the source of the irritation, it may be necessary to take the dog in for allergy testing. It is possible your pet will need antihistamines to provide relief and stop the chewing and scratching.

Signs of Illness

Any of the following symptoms may indicate the presence of a more serious medical problem. If your dog exhibits any of these behaviors, you should have the animal evaluated immediately. Delay may allow a condition that could be treated and resolved to become chronic.

Heartworms

Heartworms are thin, long worms that live in the cardiac muscle and cause bleeding and blocked blood vessels. The presence of these parasites can lead to heart failure and death. Coughing and fainting, as well as an intolerance to exercise, are all symptoms of heartworm.

The parasite, *Dirofilaria Immitis*, is transmitted by a mosquito bite. You should discuss heartworm prevention with your vet and, together, decide on the best course of action to keep your pet safe.

Bad Breath and Dental Care

While bad breath or halitosis is not a health problem per se, it can be an indication of dental issues, like an over-accumulation of plaque or periodontal disease like gingivitis. Regular dental exams by the vet and brushing your pet's teeth daily will help to prevent these problems.

Your vet's office should carry "finger brushes," canine-specific toothpaste, and dental chews. Using these products does not replace regular dental cleanings, but they are very helpful. Ask your vet to demonstrate the proper way to brush your dog's teeth, and start early. Puppies are much more agreeable to the process than older dogs.

Other problems that may lead to bad breath include sinus infections, canine diabetes, tonsillitis, respiratory disease, kidney disease, liver disease, gastrointestinal blockages, and even cancer. Always consult with your vet in instances of chronic and unresolved halitosis.

Other Warning Signs

In addition to these warning signs of potential illness, also be on the lookout for:

- Excessive and unexplained drooling
- Excessive consumption of water and increased urination
- Changes in appetite leading to weight gain or loss
- Marked change in levels of activity
- Disinterest in favorite activities
- Stiffness and difficulty standing or climbing stairs
- Sleeping more than normal
- Shaking of the head
- Any sores, lumps, or growths
- Dry, red, or cloudy eyes

Often the signs of serious illness are subtle. Again, trust your instincts. You know your dog. If you think something is wrong, do not hesitate to consult with your vet.

Anal Glands

If your Jug has an episode of diarrhea, or if the animal's stools tend to be soft, the sacs on either side of the anus, the anal glands, may become blocked and foul smelling.

Signs that a dog has blocked anal glands typically include scooting or rubbing the bottom on the ground or carpet.

If this occurs, the glands will need to be expressed to prevent an abscess from forming. This is a sensitive task and one that a veterinarian should perform.

Chapter 8 - Showing Your Jug

Unfortunately, the Jug dog breed has not been recognized by the American Kennel Club as an individual breed because it is a hybrid of two existing breeds. This means that the Jug is not eligible for competition at AKC shows.

The Jug breed is, however, eligible for registration with the International Designer Canine Registry (IDCR), and you may be able to find breed-specific shows in which to enter your Jug dog.

The Scruffts National Crossbreed Competition

If you live in the United Kingdom, your Jug dog may be eligible to compete in Scruffts, the national crossbreed competition. This competition is designed for crossbreed dogs – that is, dogs whose parents are of two different breeds or a mixture of several different breeds.

The name Scruffts is a play on words referencing Crufts, the world's largest dog show that is also sponsored by the UK Kennel Club each year.

The Scruffts dog show is less formal than Crufts, but it is still a great place to showcase your Jug dog. Each year, the UK Kennel Club holds Scruffts heats all over the UK to find the dogs that are best suited for the competition. The winners from each heat are then invited to participate in the Discover Dogs event in London for the Class Finals.

Some of the titles that dogs in the Scruffts show compete for include the following:

- "Most Handsome Dog" – for male dogs aged 6 mo. to 7 years.

- "Prettiest Bitch" – for female dogs aged 6 mo. to 7 years.
- "Child's Best Friend" – for dogs 6 mo. to 12 years, handled by a child aged 6 to 16 years.
- "Golden Oldie" – for dogs 8 years or older
- "Best Crossbreed Rescue"
- "Good Citizen Dog Scheme Crossbreed Class"

The Scruffts dog show was first held in 2000, but it wasn't until 2013 that it was held in conjunction with Crufts. The show is meant to provide the owners of mixed breed dogs with an opportunity to experience conformation competition.

What to Know Before Showing

Though crossbreed dog shows are less formal than major shows like Crufts and the Westminster Dog Show, that doesn't mean you can't still take them seriously. In this section, you will receive some valuable tips for preparing your Jug dog for show.

In order to attend a dog show, your Jug should meet the following general criteria – though these rules may not be set forth by the competition, they are generally recommended for the safety of your dog, yourself, and others:

- Your dog should be properly housetrained.
- Your dog should be properly socialized and capable of interacting safely with other dogs and people.
- Your dog should respond to basic commands such as sit, stay, and come.
- Your dog should listen and pay attention to you, even in the presence of distractions.
- Your dog should not be overly excitable or unmanageable in exciting situations.
- Your dog should meet the age requirements for the competition (generally a minimum of 6 months).

- Your dog should be properly vaccinated.

Photo: Sergei by Mercedes Clark-Smith

What to Bring to the Show

If your dog meets all of the requirements above, you can move on to thinking about what kind of preparations you need to make for the show. Take the time to read as much information as you can about the show, including registration requirements, fees, location information, and more.

The more you know about the competition, the better prepared you will be. You should also plan what you are going to take to the competition so you have what you need in case of an emergency. Below you will find a list of supplies to bring to a dog show:

- Dog crate or kennel
- Exercise pen
- Grooming table
- Grooming supplies
- Towels
- Food and treats
- Food and water bowl
- Water for the dog
- Trash bags
- Change of clothes
- Registration information

Make sure you have a good relationship with your Jug – this will help you keep him under control during the show.

Practice with your dog as much as you can – this includes running through your routine and making sure your Jug is used to spending time around other dogs.

Plan ahead when packing for your first show – make a list and check the list twice before you set out.

Read and re-read the rules and regulations for each show, so you don't accidentally disqualify your dog.

Arrive at the venue early, so you have time to unpack and look around a little bit.

Remember that it is just a show – if your Jug doesn't win, it isn't the end of the world; you still had fun and you got to spend some quality time with your dog.

Chapter 9 - Preparing for Older Age

It can be heartbreaking to watch your beloved pet grow older – he may develop health problems like arthritis, and he simply might not be as active as he once was.

Unfortunately, aging is a natural part of life that cannot be avoided. All you can do is learn how to provide for your Jug's needs as he ages so you can keep him with you for as long as possible.

Photo: Sergei by Mercedes Clark-Smith

What to Expect

Aging is a natural part of life for both humans and dogs. Sadly, dogs reach the end of their lives sooner than most humans do.

Once your Jug reaches the age of 8 years or so, he can be considered a "senior" dog.

At this point, you may need to start feeding him a dog food specially formulated for older dogs, and you may need to take some other precautions as well.

In order to properly care for your Jug as he ages, you might find it helpful to know what to expect. On this page, you will find a list of things to expect as your Jug dog starts to get older:

- Your dog may be less active than he was in his youth – he will likely still enjoy walks, but he may not last as long as he once did, and he might take it at a slower pace.

- Your Jug's joints may start to give him trouble – check for signs of swelling and stiffness and consult your veterinarian with any problems.

- Your dog may sleep more than he once did – this is a natural sign of aging, but it can also be a symptom of a health problem, so consult your vet if your dog's sleeping becomes excessive.

- Your dog may have a greater tendency to gain weight – this is particularly common in small breeds like Jack Russell Terriers and Pugs, so you will need to carefully monitor his diet to keep him from becoming obese in his old age.

- Your dog may have trouble walking or jumping – Pugs in particular tend to develop nerve degeneration as they age, so keep an eye on your Jug if he has difficulty jumping, or if he starts dragging his back feet.

- Your dog's vision may no longer be as sharp as it once was – pugs are particularly prone to developing cataracts and PRA in old age, so your Jug may be predisposed to these problems.

- You may need to trim your Jug's nails more frequently if he doesn't spend as much time outside as he once did when he was younger.

- Your dog may be more sensitive to extreme heat and cold, so make sure he has a comfortable place to lie down both inside and outside.

- Your dog will develop gray hair around the face and muzzle – this may be less noticeable in Jugs with a lighter coat.

While many of the signs mentioned above are natural side effects of aging, they can also be symptoms of serious health conditions. If your dog develops any of these problems suddenly, consult your veterinarian immediately.

Caring for an Older Dog

When your Jug gets older, he may require different care than he did when he was younger.

Both Jack Russell Terriers and Pugs are prone to developing certain diseases and conditions as they age, so you can expect your Jug to develop some of these things as well.

The more you know about what to expect as your Jug ages, the better equipped you will be to provide him with the care he needs to remain healthy and mobile.

Here are some tips for caring for your Jug dog as he ages:

- Schedule routine annual visits with your veterinarian to make sure your Jug is in good condition.

- Have your vet perform a body condition evaluation – both Pugs and Jack Russell Terriers are prone to obesity in old age, so you need to keep an eye on your Jug's body weight.

- Consider switching to a dog food that is specially formulated for senior dogs – a food that is too high in calories may cause your dog to gain weight.

- Supplement your dog's diet with DHA and EPA fatty acids to help prevent joint stiffness and arthritis – both Pugs and Jack Russell Terriers are prone to these problems as they age.

- Brush your Jug's teeth regularly to prevent periodontal diseases, which are fairly common in older dogs.

- Continue to exercise your dog on a regular basis – he may not be able to move as quickly, but you still need to keep him active to maintain joint and muscle health.

- Provide your Jug with soft bedding on which to sleep – the hard floor may aggravate his joints and worsen arthritis.

- Use ramps to get your dog into the car and onto the bed, if he is allowed, because he may no longer be able to jump.

- Consider putting down carpet or rugs on hard floors – slippery hardwood or tile flooring can be very problematic for arthritic dogs.

In addition to taking some of the precautions listed above in caring for your elderly Jug, you may want to familiarize yourself with some of the health conditions your dog is likely to develop in his old age.

Elderly dogs are also likely to exhibit certain changes in behavior, including:

- Confusion or disorientation
- Increased irritability
- Decreased responsiveness to commands
- Increase in vocalization (barking, whining, etc.)
- Heightened reaction to sound
- Increased aggression or protectiveness
- Changes in sleep habits
- Increase in house soiling accidents

Jugs are generally fairly even-tempered, but as they age, they may start to develop some of the trickier traits of their parent breeds. Pugs, for example, can be fairly jealous of other dogs and even children in the house.

As your Jug ages, these tendencies may increase – he may also become more protective of you around strangers.

Jack Russell Terriers have a tendency to develop "small dog syndrome" and may not always listen to commands – as your Jug gets older, you may find that he responds to your commands even less frequently than he used to.

The most important thing you can do for your senior dog is to schedule regular visits with your veterinarian. You should also, however, keep an eye out for signs of disease as your dog ages.

The following are common signs of disease in elderly dogs:

- Decreased appetite
- Increased thirst and urination
- Difficulty urinating/constipation
- Blood in the urine
- Difficulty breathing/coughing
- Vomiting or diarrhea
- Poor coat condition

If you notice your elderly Jug exhibiting any of these symptoms, you would be wise to seek veterinary care for your dog as soon as possible.

Euthanasia

End of life decisions for our pets are some of the toughest choices any animal lover can make. No one can or should tell you what to do in this regard.

At those times when I have had to make the choice to aid a pet into a peaceful and pain free transition, I have been extremely fortunate to have the advice and counsel of veterinary professionals who cared about me as well as my animal.

I can't emphasize strongly enough how important it is to have a vet you trust and with whom you can talk. My vet cared for me as much as she cared for my dogs and cats, and knew that I had one criterion in making my health care decisions — is the animal suffering, and is there anything you can do to help?

I will confess I have gone to financial extremes in caring for my animals, and I have witnessed others do the same.

For the most part, our pets don't know when they have a fatal illness, nor do they mourn the passing of the years as we humans do. The great gift of their existence is a life lived completely in the present — and completely present. We often suffer far more than they do.

You must make the best decision that you can for your pet, but from my perspective, that last decision, to relieve the suffering of a beloved pet at the end of his life, is a great act of love. I think they know that.

When the time comes, euthanasia, or putting a dog "to sleep," will usually be a two-step process.

First, the veterinarian will inject the dog with a sedative to make them sleepy, calm, and comfortable.

Second, the veterinarian will inject a special drug that will peacefully stop their heart.

These drugs work in such a way that the dog will not experience any awareness whatsoever that their life is ending. What they will experience is very similar to falling asleep, or what we humans experience when going under anesthesia during a surgical procedure.

Once the second stage drug has been injected, the entire process takes about 10 to 20 seconds, at which time the veterinarian will then check to make certain that the dog's heart has stopped.

There is no pain with this process, which is a very gentle and humane way to end a dog's suffering and allow them to peacefully pass on.

We humans are often tempted to delay the inevitable moment of euthanasia, because we love our dogs so much and cannot bear the thought of the intense grief we know will overwhelm us when we must say our final goodbyes to our beloved companion.

Unfortunately, we may regret that we allowed our dog to suffer too long, and find ourselves wishing that we humans had the option to peacefully let go when we reach such a stage in our own lives.

Grieving a Lost Pet

Some humans have difficulty fully recognizing the terrible grief involved in losing a beloved canine friend.

There will be many who do not understand the close bond we humans can have with our dogs, which is often unlike any we have with our human counterparts.

Your friends may give you pitying looks and try to cheer you up, but if they have never experienced the loss of such a special connection themselves, they may also secretly think you are making too much fuss over "just a dog."

For some of us humans, the loss of a beloved dog is so painful that we decide never to share our lives with another, because the thought of going through the pain of such a loss is unbearable.

Expect to feel terribly sad, tearful, and yes, depressed, because those who are close to their canine companions will feel their loss no less acutely than the loss of a human friend or life partner.

The grieving process can take some time to recover from, and some of us never totally recover.

After the loss of a family dog, first you need to take care of yourself by making certain that you remember to eat regular meals and get enough sleep, even though you will feel an almost eerie sense of loneliness.

Losing a beloved dog is a shock to the system that can also affect your concentration and your ability to find joy or be interested in participating in other activities that are a normal part of your daily life.

Other dogs, cats, and pets in the home will also be grieving the loss of a companion and may display this by acting depressed, being off their food, or showing little interest in play or games.

Therefore, you need to help guide your other pets through this grieving process by keeping them busy and interested, taking them for extra walks, and finding ways to spend more time with them.

Wait Long Enough

Many people do not wait long enough before attempting to replace a lost pet and will immediately go to the local shelter and rescue a deserving dog. While this may help to distract you from your grieving process, this is not really fair to the new fur member of your family.

Bringing a new pet into a home that is depressed and grieving the loss of a long-time canine member may create behavioral problems for the new dog that will be faced with learning all about their new home, while also dealing with the unstable energy of the grieving family.

A better scenario would be to allow yourself the time to properly grieve by waiting a minimum of one month to allow yourself and your family to feel happier and more stable before deciding upon sharing your home with another dog.

Photo Credit: Jimtography

Managing Health Care Costs

The estimated annual cost for keeping a medium-sized dog, including required health care, is around $650 / £387.

There is, of course, no possible way to estimate the cost of emergency care, advanced procedures, or consultations with specialists.

For this reason, there is a growing interest in pet insurance to help defray the costs of veterinary care. Treatments for our pets are growing in both sophistication and rate of success, but as is the case with human medical care, the costs can be high.

It may be possible to obtain comprehensive pet insurance including coverage for accidents, illness, and even some hereditary and chronic conditions for as little as $25 / £16.25 per month. Benefit caps and deductibles vary by company.

Bonus Chapter 1 - Interview with Mercedes Clark-Smith

I hope you have enjoyed reading this guide on Jug dogs, and we are not quite finished yet. This extra section is an interview which I did with owner Mercedes Clark-Smith, owner of Sergei, who is pictured extensively in this book.

Mercedes, perhaps we could start by you telling us how long you have been a Jug owner?

Sergei is 4 and we've had her since she was 12 weeks old. We looked at quite a few Jug puppies before we chose her - there was something just a bit different about her as she's a cross between a black Pug and a wire-haired Jack Russell.

How much did Sergei cost to buy?

She was the last in the litter and reduced for a quick sale so a bargain £150. When we were looking, the average cost was around £250-£300 a puppy.

Where did you buy her from?

A lady who bred from her pet JRT in Swansea, United Kingdom. We were very careful to meet both parents and ensure it wasn't a front for imported or puppy farm puppies, and we saw her with her brothers and sisters.

It was very clear the lady loved her dog to bits – she even showed us photos of mum winning prizes at the local dog show. She'd had the puppies checked by a vet, with their first vaccinations done, and she gave us a blanket that smelled of Sergei's mum to take home with us, along with a couple of days food so Sergei's tummy wouldn't be upset by a change of diet.

Do you have any advice to potential new buyers/owners?

Jugs do end up as rescue dogs, so I would say check with your local dog rescue before looking to buy a puppy. I suspect because they are little and have a lot of pug traits like a love of people and big sad eyes.

People get them thinking they will be handbag dogs and then can't cope with them when they turn out to be quite robust little hounds.

In my experience, Jugs are still 50% terrier with lots of energy, curiosity, and penchant for naughtiness. Certainly never buy a Jug on the Internet and always ask to see the parents. If you have any doubts, walk away.

Has Sergei had any health issues?

None – generally Jugs seem to be quite robustly healthy. She does snort a little like a Pug sometimes, but the vet advises it's nothing to be concerned about. She is walked in a harness though as it seems to be more comfortable for her than a collar and lead.

Why do you think people should choose the Jug over another breed of dog?

We wanted a Pug but were concerned about the breed's health issues. Then one day, in a supermarket car park, we saw a man with a type of dog we'd never seen that was clearly full of personality and that set us on the path to finding out more about Jugs.

Sergei really is the best of both – she's got all the energy, robustness and smarts of a terrier, combined with a love of people and cuddles. She loves her walks as much as she loves her bedtime!

As a cross breed, Jugs do vary in size but generally they are quite small so very suitable for most families and, if socialised as puppies, can happily get on with other dogs.

Sergei's playmate when she was a puppy was a Great Dane, so she clearly doesn't think of herself as little.

What would you say are common mistakes that you have seen Jug owners make?

I think a lot of dog owners forget small dogs are still dogs. They need exercise, mental stimulation (this is very true of Jugs as their terrier side can be destructive if bored), training, and veterinary care.

What are your routines such as how often and what types of food do you feed Sergei?

I'm not sure there is specifically for Jugs but she's fed twice a day with good quality wet food & mixer (Lily's kitchen), the occasional meal of pilchards or fresh cooked meat.

Being half Pug they can be prone to weight gain, so she doesn't have many treats and certainly no human food scraps.

Can you offer any tips, advice, and perhaps some accessories that you wouldn't be without?

Most Jugs are flat-coated. Sergei has a mane of coarse fur round her neck and down her back, so every so often I use a stripping tool (same as I use on our Lakeland x Border) to tidy her up, but otherwise she doesn't need any grooming.

I think Jugs are brilliant little dogs – they don't really need anything but food, exercise, and attention. They are extremely clever, so very easy to train, and they really like training and playing games with their owner or other dogs as it keeps their minds occupied. I think the thing to remember is that they are not lap dogs – they have a terrier side that some people might find challenging.

We crated Sergei overnight and when we went out when she was a puppy, just until she was housetrained and could use the dog flap. She would wake up about 2 am and cry, so I would get up to calm her and she would want to play. The only way to settle her was to put her in bed with us until she dozed off. Big mistake – 4 years on and she's never set paw in her own bed to sleep at night.

One thing though that is very like Pugs is their eyesight. Pugs eyes are unusual in that they can see more definition than most dogs and this is also true of Jugs. Sergei can spot pictures of a dog on TV from the other side of the room and will fling herself at the TV – so maybe the advice is to make sure your TV is secure on its stand!

Thanks so much, Mercedes for sharing your expertise.

Bonus Chapter 2 - Interview with Little Rascals Breeders

In this extra interview, we find out a little bit more about Jugs from the perspective of a well-known breeder.

Can you tell us who you are and where you are based?

We are Little Rascals. We are licensed dog breeders within the county of Lincolnshire, United Kingdom. We pride ourselves as leading the way with making sure all our puppies have the utmost care prior to leaving us to their new homes and offer an after-care support to all their new owners.

We have been breeding dogs for nearly 50 years and have an extensive knowledge base within our Kennel team, and we specialise in small-breed pedigree and cross-breed dogs.

As a breeder of Jugs in the UK, can you tell our readers a bit about the history of how Jugs came about in the UK and what you know about their development elsewhere in the world?

The Jug came by the increasing concern over the well-being of the pug over their breathing. By crossing the pug with a long-nosed alternative breed, it has seen an increase of ability to breath.

With crossing with the Jack Russell, it has been a breed of choice as it decreases the size and increases their energy level for the more active family.

Are Jugs likely to become more popular would you say – where do you see the breed heading?

Here at Little Rascals we see that there will always be a place for this hybrid puppy as they are a loveable, loyal breed.

How much do Jugs typically cost?

Our puppies are sold for £450 ($750).

What is their expected lifespan on average?

12 to 15 years.

littlerascalsuk.com

How would you describe a 'typical Jug' – what can owners expect of a Jug?

They are a lovely family pet that is full of energy and lots of character. They have the strong personality of the Jack Russell with the loving of the Pug.

What about health concerns in breeding a hybrid dog – are there specific issues that could occur with a Jug?

With the Jack Russell breed being within the hybrid, this brings the nose of the Pug out, which enables them to breathe more freely.

As with all reasonable breeding, the parents must be without any ailments related to either breed. The common ailment to look out for is overshot jaws, which may not cause any issues with the puppies. All puppies should be checked via a vet prior to going to their new home.

Do they require any special attention, needs, or diet?

Here at Little Rascals we have not experienced any issue with their diet as the Jack Russell is a hardy breed and makes the Jug a strong breed.

What are the advantages of choosing to own a Jug?

The Jug is great for a family that are always out and about. They are agile, strong dogs without the health issues that can come from owning a pedigree pug. This dog is good for a first-time dog owner due to the low risk of any health issues.

Thank you to Little Rascals for providing this interview.

http://www.littlerascalsuk.com

Bonus Chapter 3 - Emma Fisher & James Lawrence Interview

Your Jug is quite a well-known one with plenty of social media attention and publicity. He's a cute one, can you tell us his name and how old he is?

Grandmaster Flash Puppy Vuiton the second.

Why the name?

We originally wanted a pair of dogs called Grandmaster Flash and Melle Mel as I thought that was a good name for a pair of dogs. We ended up just getting one so stuck with Flash for short.

We do intend to get Melle Mel (Mel for short) at some point too. The Puppy Vuiton bit was a nickname a friend of mine had for another dog James used to have called Max. Since he was Puppy Vuiton, we figured Flash should be the second. Simple really!!

How did you come to decide to buy a Jug; had you even heard of them at the time?

We originally looked at Pugs after falling in love with a friend's, but we were worried about their breathing issues, then I came across a picture of a Puggle on Pinterest and fell in love, so we started looking at Puggles. There weren't many Puggle puppies in Sheffield (United Kingdom) at the time, and our search lead us to Jugs and we absolutely fell in love.

Where did you buy him from and how much for if you don't mind us asking?

We found a breeder advertising on the pets4homes website and he was £350.

How did the buying process work – I'm sure new owners may be concerned about this?

We went to see lots of puppies (which was fun in itself) all across South Yorkshire, and there are lots of really good tips online about what to do when visiting, what questions to ask, and what to look for.

Our main reason for looking at so many was that we wanted to be very sure that we were buying from a reputable breeder and we weren't funding a puppy farm and I'll be honest, a couple of the places we visited we weren't comfortable buying from. But we luckily found our breeder, she clearly loved dogs and knew a lot about both breeds.

The key is to make sure you meet the parents, see how they are with the puppies, with you, with the family that they are with.

Most people can tell when a dog is happy, and Flash's parents were very happy and friendly too. The main tip I'd say is to make sure the person you're buying from is as interested in you as you are in them, as they are more likely to be a responsible breeder. In the end though, Flash definitely chose us rather than us choosing him.

Does he attract a lot of interest being an unusual breed?

Loads, but we're not sure if it's because of the breed or that he's so cute. Where we live there are quite a few Jugs, so people do know what he is, but outside of the area, they seem to be less common – we once had a man stop the bus he was driving in Manchester to ask what breed he was and he always gets loads of compliments when we're out.

Can you offer any general advice to someone thinking of buying a Jug puppy?

Make sure you have time to spend in the house with your new puppy, and a lot of patience! The first week when he was crying all night as he wasn't used to sleeping on his own was hard. You have to be strong and leave him alone or he'll never stop. Stuffing a small travel clock in a toy is a good tip, as this simulates the mother's heartbeat for small pups and they settle more easily.

Also try to get something that smells like their mother from the breeder, who will usually provide this as standard if they are a good one.

The whole dog is for life thing is a good thing to keep in mind, as it's a complete life change getting one. You have to adjust your social life, work life, holiday plans, everything really to accommodate a new family member. So be absolutely 100% positive it's what you want, and that you are willing to commit entirely. If there's even a shadow of doubt, wait a while and maybe borrow a friend's dog for a few days to really understand what the commitment is.

Did you immediately have to go to the vets for vaccinations?

Yes, we got him jabbed straightaway at 8 weeks old, then again after another two weeks. Then there was a check up after a few months and now every 6 months that he's full grown.

Some people are concerned about crossbreeds; what is your experience, especially with health issues?

Flash has always been exceptionally healthy. We read that genetic health issues are common in pedigree dogs, as any condition is heightened by the interbreeding. Pugs were bred to have flat faces, so naturally they have issues with breathing and bulgy eyes as a result. That's not to say all pedigrees have genetic diseases, but they are more prone to them. When two breeds are mixed, since their genes are more different, the conditions tend to be less. Flash has a longer snout like a Jack Russell, so no problems with breathing. For us that was one of the reasons that we got a cross breed.

Given the Jug is a cross – what personality does Grandmaster Flash have?

He really is a Pug and a Jack Russell at once. He's got that 'grab hold of something and rag it' tendency, loves to chase sticks, balls, and anything else till he is tired out, and loves to dig for things just like any terrier would.

At the same time he's got that inquisitive nature of a Pug, as well as loving to sleep for hours on your lap, in bed, or anywhere else he can be warm and snuggly.

He can be wary of other people and dogs he doesn't know, but once he gets to know someone he'll remember them forever.

Do you have any advice on bringing him home, training, and settling into your home?

Just spending time with him was the main thing. They sleep so much when they're puppies that you just need to be around for the 5 minutes every hour when he wants to be moving around or going to the toilet.

Keeping him confined to his crate and a small area just outside his crate is a good idea at first, so he can settle into that and make it his space. Then once you do let him out, he will always have that crate to go back to and feel secure. Flash still sleeps in his crate sometimes now when he's on his own. We've never changed the basket in there, even though it's too small for him now. He also hordes his toys in there still so clearly considers it his place.

Training is just a case of patience and treats, whatever you're training him to do. At first, he won't understand about toileting outside, but you have to try and catch him before he goes inside and take him outside. Perhaps even sit outside with him until he goes, then bring him back in once he has.

Positive reinforcement in the form of treats is also a great tool. Of course there are other theories about how best to train a dog, but with Flash we found that treats as a reward worked great rather than punishment for going inside for example.

What would be the positives and negatives of owning a Jug would you say?

Positive is very simple. You have a Jug. He will become a big part of your life and family, and it's like having a baby that very quickly becomes a teenager and stays as one. Sometimes you think he's a grown up and responsible thing and then two minutes later you can't believe what he's done (rolled in something stinky mostly).

Any negatives are not negatives really, as you know them when you get him, so not having time to yourself, having to plan around him and think of his welfare is something you know beforehand and actually becomes enjoyable rather than a negative. If you don't think you like clearing up poo or not being able to stay out all night on a whim, then you probably shouldn't be getting a dog!

Do you have any special feeding routines or diet?

No, he is fed twice a day on some food that the breeder and vet said was good. He will eat pretty much anything, though we try not to give him anything that isn't natural as it is of no benefit and is more likely to upset his stomach since it's not used to it. So raw fruit and veg is fine (with the exception of fruit seeds, raisins or grapes and garlic, all of which are toxic to dogs) but we tend to limit it to that. He's a huge fan of salad food, carrots, peppers, cucumber, and tomatoes are some of his favourites.

Are there some tips and advice that you think most owners would be unaware of – utilising your personal experience of the breed?

Even though he's only a small dog, he'll walk for hours and hours if you want him to, but he is also just as happy sat on the sofa all day. As with all dogs, they need some exercise, but I think this comes down to the dog themselves rather than the breed.

Crossbreeds tend to vary amongst themselves, so whilst Flash and another Jug might be the same breed they could have different cross levels and look very different and have different traits. The fun of owning a dog is finding out what your dog likes and doesn't and taking it from there.

Thank you to Emma and James for taking the time to answer our questions.

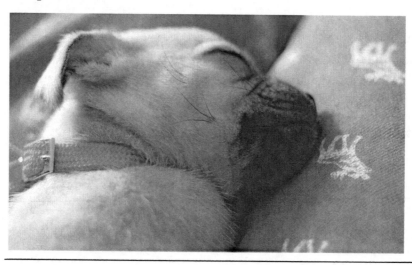

Glossary

Abdomen – The surface area of a dog's body lying between the chest and the hindquarters, also referred to as the belly.

AKC – The American Kennel Club.

Allergy – An abnormally sensitive reaction to substances including pollens, foods, or microorganisms. May be present in humans or animals with similar symptoms including, but not limited to, sneezing, itching, and skin rashes.

Anal glands – Glands located on either side of a dog's anus used to mark territory. May become blocked and require treatment by a veterinarian.

Arm – On a dog, the region between the shoulder and the elbow is referred to as the arm or the upper arm.

Artificial Insemination – The process by which semen is artificially introduced into the reproductive tract of a female dog for the purposes of a planned pregnancy.

Back – That portion of a dog's body that extends from the withers (or shoulder) to the croup (approximately the area where the back flows into the tail).

Backyard Breeder – Any person engaged in the casual breeding of purebred dogs with no regard to genetic quality or consideration of the breed standard is referred to as a backyard breeder.

Bat Ear – A dog's ear that stands upright from a broad base with a rounded top and a forward-facing opening.

Bitch – The appropriate term for a female dog.

Blaze – A white stripe of fur between the eyes.

Blooded – An accepted reference to a pedigreed dog.

Breed – A line or race of dogs selected and cultivated by man from a common gene pool to achieve and maintain a characteristic appearance and function.

Breed Standard – A written "picture" of a perfect specimen of a given breed in terms of appearance, movement, and behavior as formulated by a parent organization, for example, the American Kennel Club or in Great Britain, The Kennel Club.

Brindle - A marking pattern typically described in conjunction with another color to achieve a layering of black hairs with a lighter color (fawn, brown, or gray) to produce a tiger-striped pattern.

Brows – The contours of the frontal bone that form ridges above a dog's eyes.

Buttocks – The hips or rump of a dog.

Castrate – The process of removing a male dog's testicles.

Chest – That portion of a dog's trunk or body encased by the ribs.

Coat – The hair covering a dog. Most breeds have both an outer coat and an undercoat.

Come into Season – The point at which a female dog becomes fertile for purposes of mating.

Congenital – Any quality, particularly an abnormality, present at birth.

Crate – Any portable container used to house a dog for transport or provided to a dog in the home as a "den."

Crossbred – A dog whose sire and dam are from two different breeds.

Dam – The mother of a dog or litter of puppies.

Dew Claw – The dew claw is an extra claw on the inside of the leg. It is a rudimentary fifth toe.

Dock – To shorten the tail of a dog.

Euthanize – The act of relieving the suffering of a terminally ill animal by inducing a humane death, typically with an overdose of anesthesia.

Fancier – Any person with an exceptional interest in purebred dogs and the shows where they are exhibited.

Free Feeding – The practice of making a constant supply of food available for a dog's consumption.

Groom – To make a dog's coat neat by brushing, combing, or trimming.

Harness – A cloth or leather strap shaped to fit the shoulders and chest of a dog with a ring at the top for attaching a lead. An alternative to using a collar.

Haunch Bones – Terminology for the hip bones of a dog.

Haw – The membrane inside the corner of a dog's eye known as the third eyelid.

Head – The cranium and muzzle of a dog.

Hip Dysplasia – A condition in dogs due to a malformation of the hip resulting in painful and limited movement degrees.

Hindquarters – The back portion of a dog's body including the pelvis, thighs, hocks, and paws.

Hock – Bones on the hind leg of a dog that form the joint between the second thigh and the metatarsus. Known as the dog's true heel.

Inbreeding – The mating of two dogs that are closely related (i.e. mother to son).

Interbreeding – The mating of two dogs of different breeds.

Kennel – A facility where dogs are housed for breeding or an enclosure where dogs are kept.

Lead – Any strap, cord, or chain used to restrain or lead a dog. Typically attached to a collar or harness. Also called a leash.

Litter – A group of puppies born at the same time.

Mask – Dark coloration on the face.

Muzzle – That portion of a dog's head lying in front of the eyes and consisting of the nasal bone, nostrils, and jaws.

Neuter – To castrate a male dog or spay a female dog; to render the dog sterile, incapable of breeding.

Pedigree – The written record of a dog's genealogy going back at least 3 generations.

Prick Ear – Ears carried erect, often pointed at the tip.

Puppy – Any dog of less than 12 months of age.

Puppy Mill – An establishment that exists for the purpose of breeding as many puppies for sale as possible with no consideration of potential genetic defects.

Purebred – A dog whose dam and sire are of the same breed; both are from unmixed descent.

Rose Ear – Small ears that fold over and back revealing the burr.

Separation Anxiety – The anxiety and stress suffered by a dog left alone for any period of time.

Sire – The accepted term for the male parent.

Spay – The surgery to remove a female dog's ovaries to prevent conception.

Stud Dog – A male dog used for breeding purposes.

Whelping – Term for the act of giving birth to puppies.

Withers – The highest point of a dog's shoulders.

Wrinkle – Any folding and loose skin on the forehead and foreface of a dog.

Index

CPSIA information can be obtained at www.ICGtesting.com
Printed in the USA
LVOW10s2011141214

418784LV00031B/1320/P